NANCY GOUDIE'S SPIRITUAL HEALTH PLAN

'Nancy Goudie's practical guide to spiritual wholeness is long overdue. We commend it to all who are looking to find a deeper walk with God.' Lyndon and Celia Bowring

'I know of few people with a greater desire to know and love God than my friend, Nancy. She also has a burning passion to share that adventure with others – this is quite a book.' Sheila Walsh

'Nancy Goudie has had a heart for God for many years. The reality of her own spiritual pilgrimage is something that she longs to share with others. Nancy Goudie's Spiritual Health Plan will be a significant tool in personal spirituality.' Jim Graham, Gold Hill Baptist Church

'Every one of us, on occasion, needs a spiritual health warning and Nancy Goudie certainly provides this. But she goes further to provide guidance as to our way forward with God. Warmly commended reading.' Clive Calver, Director General, Evangelical Alliance

'I am delighted that Nancy Goudie has written this book as it brings a much needed emphasis on God's ability to heal and restore without another direct human agency.' Lynn Green, YWAM

'I have great respect for Nancy. The depth of her faith and spirituality are the genuine products of years of walking with the Lord and seeking to serve Him. That's why I recommend her writing to you.' Steve Chalke, Oasis Trust

Nancy Goudie's spiritual health plan

90 days to transform your walk with God

Nancy Goudie

Hodder & Stoughton
LONDON SYDNEY AUCKLAND

British Library Cataloguing in Publication Data
A record for this book is available from the British Library

ISBN 0 340 63062 0

Cover: Clothes by Pineapple Studios, Covent Garden, London

Typeset by Hewer Text Composition Services, Edinburgh
Printed and bound in Great Britain by
Cox & Wyman, Reading, Berks.

Hodder and Stoughton Ltd
A Division of Hodder Headline PLC
338 Euston Road
London NW1 3BH

Dedication

I want to dedicate this book to the memory of Smith Wigglesworth (1859–1947), whose life story constantly inspires, encourages and challenges me to go deeper with God. He was a powerful man of God who not only preached about Jesus but knew Him intimately.

Contents

About the author

Nancy Goudie, along with her husband, Ray, has been in full-time Christian ministry since 1980. She became a Christian when, at the age of six, she had a very dramatic and powerful experience of God. During the first twenty-two years of her life, she attended a Brethren church in her home town of Ayr, Scotland. During her teens she became part of a well-established Christian band called Unity. As well as singing with the band, she also put her qualifications in speech (ALCM) to good use by being one of the narrators in the musicals that Unity produced.

In 1981, Ray and Nancy founded and led the internationally known band Heartbeat. As one of the singers and main speakers, she travelled and ministered throughout the UK and abroad and saw many young people being touched by the power of God. Since Heartbeat's ministry finished in 1991, her gifts of preaching and teaching have been used not only in Britain but also in mainland Europe and the USA. She has also been interviewed on radio and television numerous times about her faith in God.

In 1992, Nancy released her first book, *Developing Spiritual Wholeness*, and as a result has been invited to lead many 'workshops' aimed at encouraging people to have a closer walk with God. As well as having an itinerant ministry, she is also part of the eldership team at her local church in Bristol.

Nancy and her husband Ray have one son, Daniel, and are currently the directors of the pioneering youth ministry, New Generation Ministries. They have four teams/bands working with them in evangelism, discipleship and church planting.

Acknowledgments

I am deeply grateful to the following people for the way they have helped me in the preparation of this book.

To the **administration staff** at NGM who have helped me with this book. Thank you for all your help – I would never have made the deadlines without you. I particularly want to thank **Ally Dormer**, our PA, for her tremendous support and hard work. Ally, you are wonderful! Your help even in the small things does not go unnoticed.

To our special friends **Neil and Zoe Edbrooke** for all your love, advice, encouragement and practical help you gave me throughout the writing of this book. You have helped me in so many ways with this book. Thank you so much for all you've done. It would have been much harder for me, had I not had your support and care.

To **all at NGM** who tried and tested my programmes. Your comments were extremely helpful.

To **James Catford** at Hodder and Stoughton for all your tremendous support and encouragement throughout this project.

To many at **Bristol Christian Fellowship** (our local church) and **Kyle Community Church** (our 'home' church in Scotland) who have prayed for this project. It was so good to know I could depend on your prayers.

To my **mum and dad** whose constant prayer support throughout my life and throughout this project has been invaluable.

To my best friend and husband, **Ray**, whose help, advice, inspiration, creative ideas, wisdom and encouragement are a constant blessing. I know that without your loyal support and encouragement, I would never have written this book.

To my very special eight-year-old son, **Daniel**. I am so grateful to God for you. Thank you for the love and sense of fun you bring into our lives. You are the best – I love you so!

And finally, to my **Heavenly Father** whose love and faithfulness throughout the years overwhelms me. Thank you for giving me vision for this book and for making that vision become reality. My prayer is that you will use what you have given me in this book, to bring many people into a deeper and more intimate walk with you.

Foreword

Nobody can deny that in the Westernised world we live in a culture of instant gratification. Several generations of consumerism have conditioned our minds to want it all, and to want it now. The social thermometer of the National Lottery shows that our materialism has shot to fever pitch – we want extravagant rewards instantly and for minimal effort.

Living as a disciple of Jesus Christ is a great challenge in such an atmosphere. The word disciple has a warm feeling about it although the word derived from it 'discipline', unhelpfully calls up images of strict school teachers or harsh parents. Yet we do not question the discipline of the disciples of the hundred metres' sprint, the marathon or the long jump. There can even be a certain romance about rising at 5 a.m. every day to run ten miles before breakfast, if the vision of an Olympic medal in a cheering stadium beckons in the imagination!

Yet a far better reward and a far greater cheering crowd awaits the disciples of Jesus Christ, if we are willing to sign up on his training programme. We find it much easier to conceive of physical training (though most of us only get as far as buying the outfit!) than spiritual or mental training. The Bible, however, teaches that the greatest race we run is not with flesh and blood muscles, but with spiritual and mental ones. The apostle Paul teaches his disciples in Rome not to be conformed to this world but to be transformed by the renewal of their minds. He tells his disciples in Corinth to take captive every thought and make it obedient to Christ. He tells the Colossian believers to fix their minds on things above, where Christ is; in fact the very point of all the scriptures is to teach us about God's ways, so that we can, as it were, think his thoughts, as far as that is possible for a human being.

I do not know about you, but in this present age I need every bit of help I can get to renew my mind. We are constantly bombarded by the most sophisticated thought-shaping technology ever known to mankind: film, TV, radio, video games, billboards, magazines, and now 'virtual reality' machines offering fantasy worlds of the senses on demand. We all like to think that we have made up our own minds about right and wrong, good and evil, and so on, but the truth is that all of us have been thoroughly brain-washed.

Not only that, but media saturation has reduced our attention span dramatically. Programme makers deliberately change video images no less than once every four seconds, both to keep our attention and to stop us from switching channels out of boredom!

Against this background I believe that Nancy's book is just the kind of thing that we need to help us to establish an 'alternative mind'. By this I mean a mind that is not slave to advertising campaigns, or the dodgy philosophies, muddled doctrines and downright exploitative strategies of entertainment and marketing moguls or political manipulators. The alternative mind is the one which is being renewed daily by feeding on that which is true and good and right, and the only trustworthy source of such nourishment is the Word of God.

I have known Nancy and her husband Ray since before they left their jobs to venture out and give all their time to serve the needs of young people. What she has to say is drawn from a deep well of experience and out of the integrity of many years of giving sacrificially as a friend and encourager to thousands of young people.

If you know that you need help achieving better spiritual fitness and in becoming better equipped to help others, then this book is both practical and accessible – and fun to use!

Graham Kendrick
1995

1 Keeping spiritually fit

It was quite incredible. I'd never seen anything quite like it before. An en-suite bedroom with a double jacuzzi bath complete with cushions on either side! Some time ago, close friends of ours invited my husband Ray, our son Daniel and myself to spend a holiday with them in the Lake District. They booked us into a wonderful hotel which had its own leisure facilities. When we arrived there, we couldn't believe our eyes. The bedroom was amazing! The hotel, restaurant and facilities were just out of this world.

The next day, our friends, John and Rose Lancaster, together with their family, decided to go on a bike ride and asked Ray if he wanted to join them. Ray explained that he had not been on a bike for years and didn't have any of the right clothing for mountain biking. However, as they had brought extra clothing and a bike for him, he finally ran out of excuses. They said they would only take him on a short bike ride of eight miles. Ray's response was 'EIGHT MILES!' They reassured him that they would take it easy and therefore it would be no problem to him. As Daniel was only six at the time, I *volunteered* to stay behind and *suffer* in the luxury swimming pool!

Off he went, a little shakily at first but soon he was cycling like he'd done it all his life. He went down his first hill and thought to himself, 'This is going to be easy'. If you have ever been to the Lake District in England, you will know that it is a very beautiful part of the country; however, a lot of its beauty is derived from the fact that it is quite mountainous.

1

Ray was doing well until he encountered his first mountain. His legs started to seize as he struggled up the hill. John, Rose and the rest of the cycling party zoomed up to the top of the hill, where they stopped and sympathetically waited for Ray. He eventually had to get off and *push* the bike the rest of the way up. Bikers kept passing him and, as you can imagine, he felt extremely embarrassed at being so unfit. When he got there, he discovered to his horror another hill just around the corner.

What a nightmare! Ray said there were times throughout the bike ride when he felt he was going to be sick. At other times he just wanted to lie down and die, or to cry because he felt so ill. On numerous occasions he felt like giving up. The only time he felt exhilarated was when he was going downhill! After what seemed like an eternity, Ray asked, 'How many more miles is it until we finish?' He then discovered that they had actually got lost and were having to cycle the long way round and cross over some of the biggest mountains.

Meanwhile, Daniel and I, after a leisurely swim, were sitting in a café waiting for the others to arrive. We were just contemplating chocolate cake and coffee when John, who had cycled on ahead, came in and asked me if I would go in the car to pick Ray up. He told me not to worry and said, 'We've done a few miles more than we had anticipated and Ray's completely exhausted.' When I picked Ray up in the car, he looked as though he couldn't move another muscle although there was just a small hint of accomplishment etched on his face. I later discovered that he had cycled, walked and almost crawled twenty-four miles! Now I understood why they had booked us a room with a jacuzzi bath!

GET FIT!

Ray's experience reflects what it's sometimes like in our Christian life. When it comes to problems in our lives, they can often seem like a big hill or even a mountain in front of us. How are we going to cope? How are we going to get over this problem? If Ray had been exercising regularly on a bike then the hills would not have seemed so much of a problem. All our friends zoomed to the top of the hill because they were fit and healthy. It may have taken more out of them than a smaller hill, but it wasn't nearly as difficult for them as it had been for Ray. I dread to think how I would have coped, if they had taken me!

Similarly, if we are exercising our spiritual life regularly then the problems and difficulties that we come across will not seem as hard. It's important to exercise physically but so much more important to exercise spiritually. I have to say that even though Ray found this bike ride difficult, he wouldn't have missed it for the world and it has given us both a keen desire to go biking more regularly. Try exercising spiritually and it will give you a deeper desire to get to know God and will also affect those who are looking on!

Gerald Coates, an international speaker from Britain, once said in his inimitable style, 'Only a fool of enormous proportions would not recognise that God is birthing something in Heaven for our nation at this time.' There is no doubt about it in my mind that God is doing a new thing across the nations of the world today. We are seeing what many people have prayed about for so long. Many churches are experiencing God stirring them to pray with loud groans as if in labour as He calls His people to join with Him in birthing a fresh outpouring of His Spirit. The armies of Heaven have been commissioned and sent out and we are experiencing a great outpouring of the Holy Spirit upon the earth. I believe we are on the verge of seeing thousands of people turn back to God.

Signs of revival in the Church are taking place and we await a great awakening in the nations of the world. It's exciting to note, as this book goes to print, that the up-to-date figures tell us that every day across the world, 102,000 people are becoming

Christians. Isn't that fantastic? Even as you read this book, 102,000 people will become Christians today. There are more people becoming Christians now than at any other point in history. Although that is so exciting, I believe God is going to do so much more. It's so important to be spiritually fit so we can be an effective part of what God is doing at this time.

In 1981, Ray and I started the work of Heartbeat, which eventually became known as New Generation Ministries, and since that time God has continued to develop our ministry in reaching a new generation for God. We now have four teams/bands (65dBA; re:fresh; Rhythmworks and Jimmy Ragstaff) as well as Ray and myself working in evangelism, discipleship and church planting. We also have a full administration team working in our offices which are based in Bristol and we have built a new recording studio in the centre of the city. Throughout all this growth, however, the need to stay close to God and be spiritually healthy is essential. What a privilege to be part of what God is doing in these days. It's exciting to be a part of the army God is raising up to turn the nations back to Him.

WHY THIS BOOK?

It was back in 1985 when God first began to talk to us and the rest of Heartbeat, our first team/band, about revival being on His heart for Britain and many other nations of the world. One of the important things God told us was that we should prepare for what He was about to do in our nation. I am more convinced than ever that one of the preparations which is crucial to us all is the need to learn to walk in intimacy with God. Many people tell me of their desire to get closer to God and have their walk with God deepen, but they don't know how to do that. Many people ask me, 'How do you actually hear from God?' This book will help to give you the answers to this type of question. It is not

4

only a book you read, it is also a book you do. Since 1989, I have developed spiritual health programmes that you can work through to enable you to come into a deeper walk with Jesus. These unique programmes will take you into the realm of meditation, memorising, Bible study, self-help questions, paraphrasing, writing a psalm, etc. I am excited at the opportunities this book gives people to go deeper than they've ever gone before.

Another reason I have written these programmes is to help people who are struggling or who are counselling those who are struggling in their Christian walk. Many years ago, after counselling many people, I discovered that often people would look to me for the answer to their problem and not to God. Although I do believe that counsel from others is essential at times, it is important that people's dependence is on God rather than on a human source. Many times when people would come to me for help, I would go away and pray, fast and seek God for them while the counsellee would relax because they were confident that I would hear from God. After a while, I began to feel that this wasn't quite how it should be! I started to ask them if they would be prepared to pray, fast and seek God for a day about their problem. I also began to think through how they should structure their day and this is how my programmes started.

The results I got from this were quite incredible. After spending a day or so fasting and praying and working their way through a programme, they came back really excited that God had spoken to them for themselves. Some knew the answer to their problem and all I had to do was to thank God for what He had already done. With others, I discovered after reading their notes that my programmes saved me hours of counselling as it gave me a detailed account of their inner thoughts and helped me pray for them with greater understanding. However, this book is not only for those who have problems in their Christian

5

life, it's for anyone who has a hunger in their heart to learn more of God and His word and be spiritually fit.

I have had many letters since the publication of my first book telling me how much God has used the programmes to bring them into a closer walk with Him. Here's an extract from a letter which really blessed me.

I wanted to let you know that your book has ministered to me so much. I am a nineteen-year-old teenager and have spent all my teenage years in a children's home. After leaving the children's home, I found myself homeless, so for a while I lived on the streets and got involved in drugs. Throughout my life, I have been abused physically, emotionally and sexually.

After meeting some Christians, I decided to live my life for God, but I had one problem, God was not a reality to me. The church I attended was full of so much hurt and pain that instead of realising the people were not strong Christians and they were only human, I blamed God. I told him, 'If that's what Christianity is about, then I don't want it.' So much came against me that I went further and further away from God. I saw your book in a magazine and felt strongly that I should buy it which I did. I read it and did your programmes and since that day, I am glad to say your book has changed my life. Instead of looking at people, I am looking at the one and only Almighty God and I am learning to trust Him. I have now got the chance of working with the homeless people on the streets and know Jesus wants to affect their lives. I praise God for you, Nancy, for the help I and many others have received from your programmes.

A.J., Scotland

Here's another from a man in Northern Ireland:

At a time of deep depression and stress, I bought your book and decided to take a day off work and spend time doing one of your programmes. I could see myself going through life as a person of no consequence and no worth. I have scars from my childhood when I was physically abused by my mother. By doing your programme and fixing my eyes on Jesus, everything started to come into perspective. I have been really challenged about dying to self. The trouble is that circumstances often overtake me and the old feelings of rejection return. I am learning that dying to self has to happen every day, every minute, through the good times as well as the bad. As I meditate on His goodness, I realise I am really in love with Jesus.

T.M.

Here's another from a woman who found my programmes helped her to discover more of God:

It would be impossible (unless I wrote a book) for me to explain all the blessings I received by doing one of your programmes. However, let me tell you briefly that I had been seeking God about my relationship with Him. You see, I know I am privileged to walk with Him all day, every day, but felt I lacked the discipline to really listen to Him, and to be honest, I didn't know where to start. I was drawn to your book and since doing the programme it has set me on the road to learning more about our Almighty God. I thank you with sincerity of heart.

S.G., West Midlands

I trust these letters encourage you to use these programmes and discover for yourself how much God is longing for your company.

USING THE PROGRAMMES

I have also had many requests asking me if I could do some programmes which would give people 'bite-sized' portions to work through. I believe that my new programmes will give many more people the opportunity of setting time aside to develop their relationship with God. I have written each programme on a particular theme with an introductory passage to envision you into the programme. Each programme will run for seven days and gives thirty minutes of exercises for each day. You will notice that I have timed each exercise; however, the programme is designed to be flexible. Don't worry if your timing is different to what I have put down. The timings are only a guide for you. I have written thirteen programmes on a variety of subjects and should you wish to run them all together, it will take you through a three-month course.

You will also notice that at the end of each chapter I give a verse or thought for you to 'carry' with you throughout the week. Also, I may recommend a particular book which may be helpful on the theme of the week. Obviously, I am not expecting you to read the whole book in a week, but if you find the programme helpful, then the suggested book may help you further.

I have also recorded a cassette which gives people music and meditations that will help them be released into the presence of God. Do contact the NGM office for details.

Physical exercise is something that I don't find easy and yet when I've actually done it, I feel so much more relaxed and alert. Exercise is extremely good for you as it helps to release the tensions and stresses of everyday life. Similarly, spiritual exercise is good for your spiritual life and should be undertaken regularly to keep you 'fit and healthy'. It always amazes me when I read about people who will spend hours exercising and training because they are dedicated to a particular sport. They are incredibly disciplined and will willingly sacrifice hours of their time. It often makes me feel ashamed of how undisciplined I am in comparison. It is so vital to be disciplined in our Christian life. However, it is important to note that while discipline by itself will not change us, it does put us in a place where God can. We don't want to get into legalism, but neither do we want to get lazy in our walk with God. It is essential to be intimate with God and especially to have a vibrant daily friendship which keeps us aware and responsive to what He's doing today.

Once you have completed a programme, do write to me and let me know what God has said and done with you. It is so encouraging for me to receive letters telling me how God has used the programmes to bring you into a deeper walk with Him. Send letters to Nancy Goudie, New Generation Ministries, Severn Ridge, 29 Gloucester Road, Almondsbury, Bristol BS12 4HH, England.

2 The exercises

THE MEDITATION WORKOUT

One of the lost arts in the Christian world is meditation. It sounds dodgy because we associate it with Transcendental Meditation or the New Age movement, but the art of meditation has actually been stolen from us. Christian meditation is a wonderful refreshing way of hearing God speak to you and has been used since the beginning of time. The Bible has many references to meditation. Let me give you a few scriptures that you can look up for yourself to discover that meditation is completely Biblical. Joshua 1:8; Psalm 48:9; Genesis 24:63; Psalm 119:148 all tell us about meditation. Transcendental Meditation and the New Age movement tell us to empty our minds. This is very dangerous and I would never encourage anyone to do that. It allows outside influences, which are not always good, to invade our minds and affect our lives. In contrast, Christian meditation is allowing God and scripture to fill our minds. Quite a difference. It demands discipline, since our minds find it easy to wander from one subject to another; however, if you are willing to try meditation, I know you will find it a very useful and fulfilling exercise.

It was back in 1981 when I first heard about meditation. I was at a British Youth for Christ conference when Alex Buchanan, a wonderful man of God, asked us to meditate on a verse from scripture and then informed us that he would pick a couple of volunteers to share what they had received from God. I don't

11

know about you, but when preachers say they will pick a few volunteers, I start to get nervous! In this case, I was even more so, because I hadn't a clue how to meditate. I looked around me to see if there was anyone else as ignorant as me but everyone seemed to be looking intently at their Bibles. I sank really low in my chair, hoping Alex wouldn't see me to pick me and tried to pretend that I knew what to do. There was silence for a few minutes, then Eric Delve, the National Evangelist for BYFC at the time, stood up and said, 'Alex, I'm sure I'm speaking on behalf of lots of people here, but I really don't know what to do. Would you teach us how to meditate?' As relief flooded through my body, I praised God for his courage and honesty! We were then shown how to meditate and since that time I have used meditation on numerous occasions in my own special times with God. It's a wonderful way of learning what God wants to teach us through His word.

So . . . how do you meditate? Let me give you step by step instructions as to how to meditate on scripture.

HOW TO MEDITATE

1 First of all, relax – it's very easy, so don't get uptight or anxious about it. If you do, then you will find it difficult to hear anything from God.
2 Look up the suggested scripture.
3 Read it slowly.
4 Pray and ask God to speak to you through it.
5 Read it again several times.
6 Spend time thinking about what the verse says.
7 Perhaps dwell on a phrase or section of the verse, or even just one word.
8 Allow yourself to follow a train of thought, until you see something in the verse you have never seen before.

9 Write down what you get.
10 If your mind begins to wander totally off the subject, then start again.

Let me give you an example. I recently meditated on John 15:4 which says, 'Remain in me, and I will remain in you. No branch can bear fruit by itself; it must remain in the vine. Neither can you bear fruit unless you remain in me.'

Once I had read it through several times and asked God to speak to me, my attention was taken up with the last sentence. 'Neither can you bear fruit unless you remain in me.' One of my main aims in life is to produce 'fruit' in my life. I want God to use me to bring many into His Kingdom and to affect Christians' lives by bringing them closer to Him. At the same time, I want God to affect my life in such a way that the Holy Spirit and the 'fruit of the Spirit' is shown more and more so that there is less of me and more of Him. God reminded me again when I meditated on this scripture that there is nothing I can do to bring these desires to pass, other than keeping close to Him. If I remove myself from the vine, or in other words do not have a vibrant and living relationship with Jesus, then I cannot produce the kind of fruit that I would like to see happen. However, if my main priority in life is to love, serve and keep close to Jesus, then all the desires of my heart will be fulfilled. He reminded me of the verse in Psalm 37:4 which was given to both Ray and me when we were called into full-time Christian work, which says, 'Delight yourself in the Lord and he will give you the desires of your heart.' I finished my meditation by telling the Lord again that I want to be a close friend to Him. I want to be someone whom He can trust with His plans and purposes. I committed myself to a deeper walk with Him.

Although my meditation did not give any fresh insights into scripture this time, it focused my attention again upon the Lord and my relationship with Him, and it reminded me of how important it was to 'remain in Him' and stirred up more of a desire to press on and go deeper with Him. I know that as you try this kind of meditation, God will use it to strengthen and excite your walk with Him.

USING YOUR IMAGINATION

Another type of meditation is using scripture, your imagination and perhaps music to bring you deeper into the presence of God. I have often used this form of meditation either by myself or with a large audience on some of the NGM presentations. The results coming from this form of meditation have been very encouraging. At the end of the meditation, people have often been in tears, having heard from God or having been touched by God in a special way. I would encourage you to use this type of exercise and not to be fearful of using your imagination. Your imagination has been created by God; therefore He does want you to use it to His glory, rather than in self-centred and unreal fantasising.

There are a few meditations of this type throughout the book. There is a companion tape to this book available from NGM which gives you music and meditations to help you. If you use this, or a similar reflective tape along with the book, then you will get more out of these meditations. I've outlined below a meditation that I have used personally which will help you get started.

HOW TO USE YOUR IMAGINATION IN MEDITATION

Put on some worship music, preferably – which does not have any lyrics in it, and open your Bible at Mark 15 and read from verse 21 to the end of chapter 16. Then read Luke 24:44 to 49. Now I want you to close your eyes and use your imagination to

14

be part of the story. Imagine yourself to be one of the people who followed Jesus during His ministry here on earth.

The last few years with Jesus have just been tremendous. You have come to love and believe in Him. You have seen Him do incredible miracles in front of your eyes and the wisdom coming from Him is amazing. He seems to know the right thing to say in each situation. He makes you feel important and deeply loved. No one has loved you the way Jesus has. He has become a special friend. Surely He must be the Messiah, the one you've been waiting for. However, this morning you have heard news that must be wrong! Someone came to your door, and told you that Jesus was arrested last night and that the authorities were going to kill Him today. Fear and panic rise in your being. Jesus has had death threats before – surely He will just walk away from this as He has done in the past?

You begin to calm down – Jesus will do something, surely! You decide to go and see for yourself. Out in the street, everyone is talking about Jesus being arrested. You overhear snippets of conversation about Him being taken to Golgotha (the Place of the Skull where they often crucify people). You run outside the city and there you meet up with the women who cared and provided for Jesus and as you look Jesus is being laid on a cross. Everything within you screams 'NO!' as you hear the hammer knocking the nails into His hands and feet. There are many throwing insults at Jesus, mocking Him and you want to stop them, but fear and bewilderment hold you back. 'What is going on, Jesus? What is happening? What about all the plans we had for the future? You are the Messiah – come on down. Show yourself'. But Jesus remains on the cross.

At that precise moment, even though it is daytime, darkness comes over the whole land. The sun disappears as though it does not want to shine on a day like today. The women around you are weeping, the disciples, Jesus' close friends, are all confused.

This cannot be happening. Suddenly, out of the darkness, Jesus calls out, 'My God, my God, why have you forsaken me?' Then He shouts loudly, 'Father, into your hands, I commit my Spirit'. It's all over. He's dead! The friend you loved and believed in has gone. Confusion and fear are raging within you. You wait with the others until they take Jesus' body down from the cross. Together you follow them and see into which tomb they lay His body. The women decide that even though He is dead, they will still take care of His needs. Together with the women you agree to visit His tomb to anoint His body with spices after the Sabbath.

Very early on the first day of the week, you meet together and hurry towards the tomb. You talk about how you are going to get the huge stone away which they have rolled across the entrance, but decide that you won't worry about that until you arrive there. When you reach the tomb, you all notice that the stone has already been rolled away and the guards who are supposed to be watching the tomb have disappeared. 'What is happening?' you ask. You walk into the tomb and see a young man sitting there in a white robe who tells you that Jesus is alive. JESUS IS ALIVE! What does he mean? How can He be? You are bewildered and you notice that your hands are trembling. You start to run to tell His disciples, but someone stands in front of you. You look up and there standing in front of you is *Jesus*. Joy and excitement suddenly fill your being as you exclaim, 'YOU'RE ALIVE, YOU'RE ALIVE!' You fall to the ground and worship Him. He hasn't let you down. Hallelujah! Jesus is alive!

After your meditation, note down how you felt as you went through the story. Write down any lessons you have learned by being part of this story. Writing things down is often very helpful, not only at the time, as it gives you a way to assess your thoughts more clearly, but also at a later stage when you need encouragement from God. It is good to look over your notes and see what God has said to you. Thank God for His plans and purposes for your life and tell Him that you will trust Him for the future, because you know He is faithful and all powerful and will bring into being those things He has promised. Spend time praising and worshipping Him for who He is.

I'm sure as you use your imagination to bring you face to face with Jesus, you will find that the Lord will use this method of meditation to speak directly into your life and touch you in a new fresh way.

It is important to realise that because the enemy often tries to deceive us, we should always make sure that what we receive from God through meditation is consistent with scripture. Share what you receive with your pastor, spiritual leader or someone whom you respect in God. I will speak more about this in the Prayer Workout.

Here are some more exercises to help draw you closer to God.

WRITING A PSALM WORKOUT

Whenever I mentioned to the people attending one of my spiritual exercise seminars that we are all going to write a psalm, a look of horror appears on a number of faces. Looks of 'You will never get me to do that' and 'Well, that's it, I may as well give up now' are common. However, if people take the plunge and decide to go for it, then they discover 'writing a psalm' to be a new and exciting way of putting their thoughts and feelings about God on paper. The first time we did this exercise in our first team, Heartbeat, I felt exactly the same. The fact that I was surrounded by people who wrote music did not add to my confidence! However, when I put pen to paper and I concentrated on my 'Heavenly Dad', a great explosion of praise happened within me and I just wrote down what I was feeling. It doesn't need to rhyme or have fancy or flowery words. It just needs to convey your love for God in a way that reflects your personality. Try reading one of the psalms in the Bible before you start: Psalm 100 is a great psalm of praise. Here's a recent psalm of mine.

Lord, you are my dearest friend,
Someone in whom I can love and trust,
Someone who is faithful and will never let me down,
Someone who has stood with me throughout the passage of time.
How I love you so!

Your arms of love surround me and I feel safe and secure,
There's nowhere I would rather be, than living close to you.
No one else can match your love – nothing else comes close,
I would rather have you than all the tea in China,
How I love you so!

Even when times are tough and I do not understand
All that I am going through. It just does not make sense.
You come with your gentle answer – 'Just trust me anyway.'
Lord, where else can I turn? You alone have all the answers.
How I love you so!

THE PARAPHRASING WORKOUT

Here is another exercise that people shy away from and yet when they experience it they realise how much it can help you get to grips with the Bible. Sometimes we pass over the more difficult parts of the Bible and if someone asked us to explain what we have read, we wouldn't know how to go about it. Paraphrasing can really help you understand the meaning behind the words. Paraphrasing is a fancy word for using your own words to express the meaning of the passage. We need to be careful that we don't change the meaning of the passage but just express it in a

18

different manner. After you have paraphrased a piece of scripture, look up the Living Bible, which is a paraphrase of the Bible, or perhaps look up a commentary to see if you have altered the meaning at all. Try the following verse and you will see how easy it is.

Read Romans 8:1 – 'Therefore, there is now no condemnation for those who are in Christ Jesus.'

Here's what it says in the Living Bible: 'So there is now no condemnation awaiting those who belong to Christ Jesus.'

Here's my paraphrase: 'Because of all that Jesus has done for us and because we know Him as a friend, we do not need to live in guilt and shame.'

Now try writing yours.

THE MEMORISING WORKOUT

When I was a child, I was taught by my parents to memorise scripture. The memorising of scripture was fairly common then, but over the years this is a practice that seems to have diminished. There are many reasons why it is important to have scripture stored in our minds. Here are a few to encourage you.

1 God has told us to do so. Deuteronomy 11:18.
2 It helps in moments of weakness or temptation; e.g. when the enemy tempts Jesus, He fights back by quoting scripture. Matthew 4:4.
3 It is really helpful when we are sharing our faith with others. Hebrews 4:12 says that God's word is sharper than a two-edged sword.

19

4 It is helpful in finding God's direction and guidance for our lives. Proverbs 3:1–6.

The main excuse for not memorising scripture is that your memory is bad. However, I love to inform people that your memory can be trained to retain information. It's usually because of lack of use that your memory isn't working as well as it used to. The best way to memorise is to break the verse into portions. Learn the first portion first, then the first and the second together, then the first, second and third together and so on until you have completed the task.

Let's take 1 Thessalonians 5:16–18 as an example. It reads like this:

> Be joyful always; pray continually; give thanks in all circumstances, for this is God's will for you in Christ Jesus.

These verses naturally fall into phrases. So, let's take the first phrase, 'Be joyful always.' Repeat that out loud many times, then add the second phrase: 'Be joyful always; pray continually.' Again repeat it a number of times before adding the third phrase: 'Be joyful always; pray continually; give thanks in all circumstances.' Repeat the same process before adding the fourth phrase: 'Be joyful always; pray continually; give thanks in all circumstances, for this is God's will for you in Christ Jesus.'

Once you have said it all, say it over and over again until it becomes part of you. Why not try recording it again and again on to a cassette and let it play while you are doing other things? It helps to get it firmly implanted in the brain. Perhaps put it on a card or piece of paper and take it with you in order that you can review it during the day. Just because you can say something once or twice doesn't mean you have memorised it. It needs reviewing in order for it to be imprinted in your memory banks.

In these days when there is so much garbage thrown at us

from our society through the media, etc., it's so important to fill our minds with God's word. In Philippians 4:8 Paul tells us to fill our minds with whatever is true, noble, right, pure, lovely, excellent and praiseworthy, because, as you are probably aware, whatever you fill your mind with eventually begins to affect your lifestyle. That's one of the reasons why it is so important to memorise scripture.

THE FASTING WORKOUT

Most people feel the task of fasting is beyond them. How could they possibly do without food for a specific period of time? I thought that myself when I first heard about fasting. However, I have found over the years that prayer and fasting together make a very powerful combination. If you've never fasted before, let me encourage you, you will not die through fasting for a few days.

Everyone who joins NGM learns how to fast unless they cannot because of medical reasons. A few years ago we discovered that one of our new teams had decided that in order to celebrate getting through their first day without food, they would have a beanfeast at midnight. We announced to the teams that when we fast for a day on training it means consuming no food until the following morning; therefore all 'beanfeasts' were out. One girl approached Ray afterwards really upset and told him she would not sleep, and in fact would not survive the night, if she didn't eat something before going to bed. Ray assured her that she wouldn't die and in fact she came back the next day and apologised. She is not alone in thinking that if you fast more than one meal you will die. There are many people who think fasting is harmful for you. The truth is that, rather than being bad for you, fasting is extremely good for your body. When you fast, the energy that is normally used to digest, etc., is then spent in purifying the body. Fasting cleanses the bloodstream, which results in better health. It certainly makes you aware of how much we seem to be ruled in our lives by our stomachs.

Although there are many physical benefits from fasting, don't fast just because you need to lose weight. If you need to diet, then there are many good diets around which can help you lose weight in a sensible and controlled manner. Your reasons for fasting should be much deeper than the desire to lose weight.

REASONS FOR FASTING

Apart from the many reasons why it is good for our physical bodies to fast, there are also many spiritual reasons why we should fast, the main one being that Jesus expects us to fast. You only have to read your Bible to discover this to be the case. Read Matthew 9:15 and also Matthew 6:16. Fasting should not be an optional extra. When we combine prayer with fasting, God's power is released into the situations for which we are praying.

There are many people in the Bible who fasted for various reasons. Let me give you a few people and their reasons for fasting.

1 **Jesus.** Matthew 4:2; Jesus fasted before His earthly ministry started.

2 **Daniel.** Daniel 10; Daniel fasted to receive more revelation from God.

3 **David.** 2 Samuel 12:16; David fasted to plead with God to change His mind.

4 **Esther.** Esther 4:16; Esther fasted before warfare.

5 **Jehoshaphat.** 2 Chronicles 20:3; he and the whole of Judah fasted for deliverance.

6 **The leaders of the church at Antioch.** Acts 13:2; they fasted to discern more of God's will.

You may have other reasons why you should want to fast but I do hope these few inspire you.

I believe fasting constantly holds your prayer request before God even though there may be times in your busy schedule when it is difficult for you to talk to God. Also, if you are finding that you just cannot break through in one or more areas of your life, then do add fasting to your prayers. I fast regularly for many different reasons, but my main reason is that I want God to anoint me more and more for what He has called me to be and do. I have to say that since I began to fast regularly some years ago, my life has completely been changed around. It is a discipline which I would recommend to anyone, but particularly to those who want to go deeper with God.

No one finds fasting easy, because everything within you fights against it. However, the good news is that it does get easier the more you do it.

WHAT IS FASTING?

Fasting primarily means consuming no food, and perhaps even no water, for spiritual reasons, over a period of time.

There are three main ways of fasting:

a) **Partial fast**. Eating simple basic food, or liquids only.
b) **Normal fast**. No food, water only or drinks e.g. fruit juices, etc. (Do not go beyond forty days – see below.)
c) **Absolute fast**. No food or water. (Do not go beyond three days – see below.)

There are other ways of fasting that do not include food:

a) **A sleep fast**. Spending a half or whole night in prayer. Or even getting up a few hours earlier than normal to spend quality time with God.

b) **A television fast**. Deciding not to watch television for a period of time. We have often used this type of fasting when it was impossible to fast food. I'm sure if you use this type of fasting you will find it not only refreshing but also very revealing. I guess we all spend too much time sitting in front of the box.

c) **A favourite fast**. If there is a particular food or drink that you really like, then why not fast it for some time? God once told a good friend of ours to stop eating his favourite snack of Coke and crisps for a while. Ray also spends time fasting his favourite drink now and then.

You can fast and pray as an individual (Psalm 35:13), as a family (1 Samuel 31:13), as a church (Acts 13:1–3) or even as a nation (Leviticus 16:29). Some time ago, our local church, Bristol Christian Fellowship, fasted corporately for three days to seek more of God. We decided that we would ask Daniel, who was seven at the time, if he would join us. He had seen us fasting many times so he knew it meant giving up something, usually food. We asked him what he would like to give up and he decided he would like to give up sweets for the three days. It was really great to be able to fast together as a family and as a church.

HOW TO FAST

Let me give you some fasting tips:

1 Do start slowly – especially if you've never fasted before. Try cutting out one meal then increase your fasting as time goes

24

on. Don't promise the Lord that you will fast forty days if in fact you have never fasted even a meal before. Start slowly and build up.

2 If you are a young person who is still living at home with your parents, then do speak with them about your desire to fast. If your parents are not Christians and forbid you to fast, then do remember there are other ways of fasting besides going without food. Also, if you share a house with someone, then do let them know you are fasting. Not only will it let them know to be sensitive, but it will also let them know not to cook you a meal. Do remember, though, not to brag about your fasting to others (see Matthew 6:16–18).

3 If you experience headaches during the fast, this may be due to caffeine withdrawal. It is wise to cut down on coffee, tea and Coke beforehand as they all contain caffeine. It's always easier to fast *without* a headache!

4 To combat hunger pangs: fool your stomach by drinking lots of water or liquid.

5 Don't be put off by the fact that you are working. You can easily fast while working unless your job is a heavy manual one. We would never advise our teams to fast when they are on mission and have to move lots of heavy equipment. Be wise, but don't make your work your excuse.

6 Try brushing your teeth many times during the day to keep your breath fresh. If this is impossible, then use mints or breath freshener sprays.

7 If you forget you are fasting and eat something, don't lose heart. God will not stop listening to you. I remember one day when I was fasting, I ate a strawberry which we had grown in our garden. It was in my mouth half eaten when I suddenly remembered that I was still fasting. Don't give up at that point, just apologise to the Lord and keep on going.

8 Break your fast *slowly*, perhaps with fruit or a light salad.

9 Do not fast food and water for more than three days as the body cannot cope without water beyond that time.
10 Do not fast food for more than forty days as the body cannot cope beyond this time. You would need God's divine help to fast for more than forty days. If you fast for more than three days, then I would recommend getting support, help and wisdom from your spiritual leaders.

A word of warning! If you are on medication for a serious illness such as heart problems, diabetes, liver or kidney disease, then I would strongly recommend that you **do not fast without consulting your doctor**.

HOW LONG SHOULD I FAST?

Personally, I would recommend fasting regularly. Perhaps do a twenty-four or thirty-six-hour fast once a week with a longer fast as and when the Lord leads you. I have found regular fasting to be incredibly uplifting in my spiritual life as well as beneficial in my physical body. I want God to continue to help me and mould me to be more like Jesus and I've discovered that fasting is one way of giving God an opportunity of doing something deeper with me.

If you have never fasted before, then as I said above, don't decide to start with a forty-day normal fast! Try missing one meal first, then progress to two meals. Then try a twenty-four-hour fast, i.e. stopping eating after 7 p.m. one night and then miss all meals the next day and start eating again at 7 p.m. Perhaps you could then try a thirty-six-hour fast, which would mean stopping eating at 7 p.m. one night, then missing all meals the next day and breaking your fast the following morning with breakfast. It is possible to fast up to forty days, but this is an exceptionally long time and should only be undertaken if you are absolutely sure that

God has told you to do so. I would recommend that you should only take on a longer fast, and by that I mean more than three days, if you get clear guidance from God and have submitted your plans to your spiritual leaders, in order that they can help, encourage and give you wisdom throughout your fast.

I would also *strongly* recommend that you only embark on an absolute fast if you receive direct instructions from God and if your church leadership witness your call from God to do so. Do remember that an absolute fast should not go beyond three days as the body cannot cope without water beyond that time. On both the forty-day normal fast and the three-day absolute fast, we would need God's divine help in order to survive beyond these timings.

It's important to know that fasting is not intended to be a crude attempt to express our spirituality, but it is one way of coming closer to God. Please don't feel condemned by thinking that a forty-day fast is for 'spiritual giants' and that you can only manage twenty-four hours! The important thing is to be obedient to God and not simply to undertake a marathon when He may only want us to attempt a gentle jog.

HOW TO BREAK A FAST

It is important that you break your fast *slowly*. I would recommend fruit, vegetables or a light salad. Do not break a fast with food that is heavy and greasy. I know from experience that this is a very silly thing to do and upsets your system, sometimes quite badly. Do remember that the longer the fast, the more gradually you should break it. Although your stomach will have shrunk during your fast, your eyes are just as big, and the temptation is that you allow your eyes to judge how much you should eat and not your stomach. Exercise your self-control and ask God to help you come off the fast sensibly.

HOW TO GET MAXIMUM BENEFIT FROM A FAST

Spiritual and physical preparation for fasting will help you get the maximum benefit from it. If you are going on a fast which is longer than twenty-four hours, then it is important to cut down on your food intake the day before. I would suggest going on a fruit or vegetable diet during the previous day. If you are used to drinking ordinary tea and coffee, then you may experience headaches during your fast. As I already advised you in the fasting tips, in order to avoid this cut out tea and coffee a few days beforehand. A headache during your fast can greatly hinder what you would like to accomplish.

As well as preparing physically, it is very important to prepare spiritually. Before embarking on your fast, write down what you want God to accomplish in you or through you during your time of self-denial. Decide how you are going to spend your day. How much time are you going to be able to put aside for prayer, study, etc.? Decide how to structure your day and decide that nothing will get in the way. Pray and ask God for His protection on you, your family and your possessions. On a practical note make sure you have bought enough drinks for your fast day.

I've often noticed that when some people fast, they will have the attitude of 'How much can I get away with here?' The question should not be 'How little can I give up for God?' but 'How much can I give up for God?' King David said in 2 Samuel 24:24, 'I will not sacrifice to the Lord my God burnt offerings that cost me nothing.' Let's fast with a generous heart towards God, with joy and delight at serving our God. He's so worth it – isn't He? Fasting is not something that should be dreaded or seen as a punishment, but should be seen as a privilege. If we can see situations change in the unseen realm because of our fasting – isn't that a real privilege?

THE PRAYER WORKOUT

Prayer is something that we all know we should do, but sometimes find very difficult. I don't think I have ever encountered anyone who has said that they find prayer to be easy. Perhaps you think that you are the only person who struggles in this area, but that is not true. We all struggle with prayer at times. It seems that every time we start to pray, the phone will ring, or the door bell will go, or we think of a hundred and one different things we should have done. I'm sure this happens because the enemy knows how effective our prayers are and will try at any cost to keep us from communicating with Heaven. Satan knows that if he keeps us from praying then he has defeated us. It's important to recognise that our prayers do accomplish much and that communication between us and our Heavenly Father is essential.

As well as finding time to have special intimate times with God, I also try to keep my communication open with Him twenty-four hours a day. I talk to Him no matter where I am and no matter what I'm doing, even if it's a very small thing like trying to find a parking space. God is interested in the small problems we have in life as well as the big ones.

FREEDOM IN PRAYER

We should never restrict our friendship with God to ten minutes in the morning and the same in the evening. If we do, then what happens is that when you miss your 'quiet time', you feel guilty for the rest of the day and often think that nothing will go right for that day. God doesn't just want a little slot in your day, He wants a constant open friendship right through the day. It is important to set aside quality time for God, but when that is impossible one day, if you have a constant friendship with Him, then your relationship doesn't have to be 'put on hold' until the next time you can give Him quality time. You can speak to Him no matter where you are, telling Him what is going on in your life and asking for His help. When I first discovered this, a real freedom came into my walk with God. No longer was I locked into legalism but was free to have a relationship with Him no matter where I was.

Prayer is something that we all need to learn. In Luke 11:1, the disciples asked Jesus to teach them to pray. These were people who knew what it was like to pray and had been taught from their earliest that they should pray to God. Their whole nation prayed, so why did they ask Jesus *how* to pray? There must have been something different about Jesus' prayers. I believe that if we look at Jesus' prayers in the Bible we will discover that He prayed with authority and boldness which emphasised His intimate relationship with His Heavenly Father. When Jesus prayed, things happened. No wonder His way of praying was so desirable. I feel in my own life I have still so much to learn about prayer. I often echo the request of the disciples, 'Lord, teach me how to pray.' Let's learn to pray the way Jesus did. I've listed below a few things we can learn from the way He prayed.

1 **He prayed out loud**.

I'm always amazed at how many hands go up when I ask people in seminars to indicate if they 'think' their prayers rather than 'speak' their prayers. There is nothing wrong in 'thinking' your prayers; however, if you do, then it can lead to wandering thoughts, whereas 'talking' your prayers helps you to focus so much better. I would encourage you to talk your prayers as much as you can. Not only will it help you in your own time with God, but it will also help you when it comes to praying publicly. There are many of Jesus' prayers recorded for us in the Bible, therefore He must have prayed out loud, e.g. John 17, John 11:41. Even on the cross Jesus 'spoke' His prayer of forgiveness (Luke 23:34).

2 **He was intimate**.

He spoke to God as if He really knew Him and even called Him His 'Daddy'. He didn't feel He needed to use old-fashioned language to speak to God. He spoke to Him as He would to a friend. Jesus had an intimate friendship with His Heavenly Dad which had developed from the beginning of time. God wants to get to know us intimately and the only way to do that is to talk with Him often. If you wanted to develop a friendship with someone, the way you would do that is to communicate with them. If you went to someone and tried to talk with them but they ignored you, then eventually you would give up and walk away. Friendship means you need to have communication in both directions.

3 **He prayed anywhere**.

Jesus prayed at a funeral (John 11:41); in a garden (Mark 14:32); on a mountain (Matthew 14:23); in lonely places (Mark 1:35); on a cross (Mark 15:34). In other words, He prayed no matter where He was. Throughout my programmes I have suggested that you go out for a walk with God. I have often found walking and talking with God to be a good way to pray and I would encourage you to try it. I recognise that the environments around you will be vastly different depending on where you live; those in the city will see things differently to those who are in the country. However, I would encourage you no matter where you live to speak to God when you walk with Him and hear God speak to you through what you see around you. In my programmes I have often limited your walk to ten minutes because of time, but of course you can extend that time if you wish. Some people may so enjoy walking and talking with God that they spend hours with Him in this way.

4 **He was specific**.
Jesus did not pray in generalities but was specific (Luke 23:34). So often when we come to God in prayer, we pray around the issue rather than telling God exactly what we need Him to do.

5 **He was persistent**.
If you look at Mark 8:22–5 where it tells the story of Jesus praying for the healing of a blind man at Bethsaida, you will see that Jesus was persistent in His prayers. Jesus quite clearly taught us in Luke 11:5–10 and Luke 18:1–8 that we should pray and not give up.

6 **He prayed in faith**.
Jesus taught His disciples to pray with faith. Read Mark 11:22–4. There is little point in praying for a specific thing to happen if we pray without any expectation that He will do what we ask. Let's ask God to increase our faith in Him to trust Him for more.

7 **He prayed with others**.
Jesus taught His disciples how important it was to pray with others in Matthew 18:19–20. Many people, including myself, find it easier to pray with others than they do on their own. At times, Jesus asked His disciples to watch and pray with Him (Matthew 26:36–8 and Luke 9:28). One thing Ray and I discovered in our married life was how important it was to pray together. The old saying is true, 'Those who pray together, stay together.' Your relationship with your partner is much stronger if you learn to pray with one another. Ecclesiastes 4:12 tells us that 'A cord of three strands is not quickly broken'. When we bring God into the centre of our relationships they become so much stronger.

8 **He submitted to His Father's will**.

In Luke 22:42, Jesus prays to His Father in the Garden of Gethsemane and says, 'Father, if you are willing, take this cup from me; yet not my will, but yours be done.' Jesus willingly submitted to the will of the Father and in fact states quite clearly in John 4:34, 'My food is to do the will of him who sent me and to finish his work.' There will be times in our prayer life where we will pray for something and God quite clearly says 'No'. A friend of mine just recently told me of a time when she was pregnant and she and her husband had prayed and asked God to give her a natural birth. However, when it came to the time for the baby to be born, he was born by caesarean section. They were disappointed and couldn't understand why God hadn't answered their prayers. When their next child was about to be born, they again asked God if they could have a natural birth, but when the child was born it also was born by caesarean section. Again, disappointment filled them and they expressed this to a doctor who was a friend and also a Christian and who just happened to be at the birth. They couldn't believe his reply. He said, 'Well, actually, if God had answered your prayer, I reckon both your babies would have died at birth, because your pelvis is too small for a natural birth.' They then understood why God had chosen to say 'No' to their prayers. It's good to know when we pray that although God may not answer our prayers the way we want, He knows what is best!

HOW TO HEAR FROM GOD

Another barrier to prayer is that people find it hard to hear God's voice. Sometimes, because of rejection or insecurity, people can miss the voice of God and therefore their growth in Him is stunted. The first thing we need to know is that God *wants* to communicate with His children. We do not serve a God who is dead nor a God who is dumb. He loves to talk with us and get to know us better.

I am no more special in God's Kingdom than you are – God loves us all – and therefore if I can hear from Heaven then so can you. That's not to say that I always find it easy to hear from God. There are times when it can be a real struggle and sometimes it can feel as though He is just not around. It's in those times that it's important to cling on to God and persist in prayer. In Luke 18:1–8 Jesus stresses the importance of persisting in prayer.

A few years ago, I went through a period of time where I found it very difficult to hear from God or even to feel His presence around me. I had often heard of people talking of 'the dark night of the soul' and had never quite understood what they meant. I wondered whether God was displeased with me because I had done something to offend Him, so I examined myself and asked God to highlight anything wrong in me. I repented of anything and everything I could think of, but still I could not hear from Heaven or feel God around me. Eventually, I cried out to God and told Him that even if I didn't feel His presence or hear His voice, I would still hold on to Him. I felt like Peter in John 6:68 who said to Jesus, 'Lord, to whom shall we go? You have the words of eternal life.' Where else could I go? I decided, even if I didn't feel Him around me or couldn't hear His voice, to believe what the Bible tells me in Hebrews 13:5, that God will never leave me nor forsake me. In Matthew 28:20 Jesus also says, 'And surely I will be with you *always*, to the very end of the age.' Throughout many months of tears and disappointment, I could only cling on to God's word.

There were times when I got annoyed with God because I couldn't understand what He was doing. I often had to repent of my bad attitudes and ask Him for His forgiveness and tell Him that even though I didn't understand why I couldn't hear from Him, I would trust Him anyway. I think I cried more through those months than I had in all my previous years. It felt like 'a dark night of the soul'. It was in those dark days when I came to appreciate more fully friends who prayed for me and encouraged me with words that they had heard from the Lord. After a number of months, without explanation God's presence suddenly returned and once more I found it a real joy to listen and hear from God.

Listening to God is an important part of prayer and therefore it is important to learn how to tune in to Him. There are many ways that God uses to speak to us – the Bible; visions or pictures; dreams; people; sermons; prophetic words; an audible voice; a still small voice, etc.

The main thing is to let God know that you are keen to hear from Him and ask Him to teach you how to listen. I have found that many people who have said they cannot hear God speak to them actually have heard Him speak but they have not recognised His voice. When we first learn to hear from God it is a bit like 'tuning in' to a radio station. It takes time and effort to get by all the different sounds and signals you hear before you eventually find the exact programme you want. Sometimes, you feel like giving up, but when you persevere it is always worth it in the end. Listening to God can be just like that. Keep 'tuning in' to Him and don't give up, because in the end it will be worth it. If you feel you have never heard from God then one of the easiest ways of hearing God speak to you is through meditation on scripture. Why not try it and see?

CHECK OUT WHAT YOU HAVE HEARD

It is of *utmost importance* that we test everything we believe we have heard from God with His written word. God will *never* contradict what He has already said in the Bible. Do remember that although the enemy at all times wants to deceive us, we can protect ourselves by submitting our 'words from God' to our spiritual leaders. We are encouraged in 1 Thessalonians 5:21 to 'Test everything. Hold on to the good.'

THE BIBLE STUDY WORKOUT

Most people think that Bible study must only be for theologians as they are the only ones who would not be bored by it, but as a young girl from Eastbourne discovered, Bible study can be exciting. She wrote to me and said

> I spent today doing one of your programmes and I have never before got so much from studying God's word. Thank you for giving me a structure which brings the scriptures alive.
>
> J.F.

When I first started to study the Bible, I, too, was amazed at how much I enjoyed it. At school, I was never into serious study, therefore thinking of studying the Bible sounded like my worst nightmare! However, when I got into it for myself, I realised just how many pearls there were just underneath the surface waiting to be found. In my programmes, I have given you certain passages of scripture to study but have made it easier for you by asking questions. I have been really blessed preparing them, so my prayer is that you will be equally blessed doing them. Do write and let me know how you have got on.

You will also find that at times I have prepared self-help questions. These questions will help you to think through issues for yourself and also help you analyse why you feel or act the way you do. I hope you not only discover more about yourself through them, but that you also discover more about God and His ways.

Worship is not just something we do on Sundays in our church meetings, it is a *way of life*. The most important thing is not where we worship, but that we live in an attitude of worship before the Lord. It's interesting to note that 1 Kings 1:47 tells us that King David worshipped on his bed!

WORSHIP AS A LIFESTYLE

Romans 12:1 tells us to offer our 'bodies as living sacrifices, holy and pleasing to God' as this is our spiritual act of worship. In Genesis 22 we read that Abraham and Isaac went to a mountain to worship the Lord. Abraham went knowing that God had told him to sacrifice his son as a burnt offering. He came to worship God and lay down someone in his life who was extra special to him. He wasn't just coming to 'sing songs', he was coming to sacrifice. He was giving God everything and nothing was being kept back. What an example to us when we come to worship God.

My desire is that I live my life in such a way that my whole life is worship to God, and that when I do speak or sing out my praise and worship of my King, I will hold nothing back. Can I encourage you to find new depths in your praise and worship of God?

In some of my programmes, I have included time for you to praise and/or worship the Lord. As with any other time of praise and worship, the way to experience more of Him is to give yourself fully to the task. Enter into praise and worship with a joyful heart – no matter what your circumstances are.

A close friend of mine, Zoe Edbrooke, is the main worship leader at our church in Bristol. She and her husband, Neil, have been going through a really tough time. Neil has been very ill for some time and his health has been a great concern to all of us. Zoe has not only looked after their four children, but also nursed Neil and helped him through the really bleak times. I have seen her in tears many times as she has watched her husband suffer, yet she is a woman who is determined to praise God through the problems. When she leads the worship on Sundays at church, she gives it her all. She may not feel like praising, but she does it anyway with all her strength because she knows God is worthy. She is such an inspiration to me and to others around. Let's determine to praise God, despite our circumstances, because He alone is worthy.

There are many ways of praising and worshipping God which I will list for you. All of them are Biblical and I would encourage you to explore each way and add more of your own. Of course, I am sure you know that it's not the ways in themselves which are worship, but they are only an outward expression of the praise and worship we have in our hearts for God.

BIBLICAL WAYS TO EXPRESS PRAISE AND WORSHIP

1 Singing — Colossians 3:16
2 Singing in the Spirit — 1 Corinthians 14:15
3 Singing out a new song — Psalm 96:1
4 Clapping hands — Psalm 47:1
5 Raising hands — Psalm 134:2; 1 Timothy 2:8
6 Speaking — Psalm 145:6–7
7 Shouting — Ezra 3:10–15
8 Playing an instrument in worship — Psalm 150:3–5
9 Dancing — Psalm 150:4; 2 Samuel 6:14–15
10 Leaping/jumping — Acts 3:8
11 Standing — 2 Chronicles 20:19
12 Being still — Psalm 46:10

13 Bowing	2 Chronicles 20:18; Matthew 2:11; Nehemiah 8:6
14 Kneeling	Psalm 95:6–7
15 Lying prostrate	Revelation 5:14; Revelation 11:16.

Don't be afraid of trying new ways to praise and worship the Lord. If you have never sung out a 'new song' to the Lord before, then why not try it? If it makes your praise and worship times more real to you and more of a blessing to God, then that's what you want to achieve.

In 1 Kings 1:40, when all the people were celebrating their new king, it says, 'And all the people went up after him, playing flutes and rejoicing greatly, so that the ground shook with the sound.' I'm sure that their praise and worship must have been really noisy and creative. Let's make the ground shake with our praise and worship, after all, we have a King who is greater than Solomon. Let's give Him the praise He so rightly deserves.

WHAT YOU WILL NEED FOR A PROGRAMME

Before you start working on a programme, let me list a few things you will need.

1 A Bible. (All the references I have given you are from the New International Version, so it might be good to use that translation.)
2 A note pad and pen.
3 You may need a dictionary, depending on which programme you choose.
4 You may need a commentary of the Bible for some of the information needed in the Bible studies. If you don't own one, then you may be able to borrow one from your pastor or leader.

39

5 Once you have decided which programme you would like to do, look through it to see what items you need, e.g. it may help to have a praise or worship tape to help you in your praise.

6 Making sure you have a room where you will not be disturbed is essential.

7 If you are fasting at any time during your programme, then do make sure you prepare yourself beforehand. Cut down on tea and coffee and perhaps go on a fruit or vegetable diet the day before.

8 Make sure you read the chapter on your particular theme before embarking on the programme. Perhaps read it the evening before you commence. This should help you be much more focused and envisioned.

9 Do remember that the timings are only a guide. Don't worry if you take longer or complete a particular exercise quicker.

My prayer for you as you work your way through this book is that your relationship with God will become stronger and stronger. I pray as Paul prayed in Ephesians 1:18-19 that 'the eyes of your heart may be enlightened in order that you may know the hope to which he has called you, the riches of his glorious inheritance in the saints, and his incomparably great power for us who believe'. I have shared with you in this book some of my failures as well as my successes and my tears as well as my joys. I pray that as you read and complete this book, God will use it to bring you closer and deeper into Him.

3 Diving into the depths of Christ's love

I am constantly amazed by the depth of the Lord's love for me. I know I'll never fully understand just how deep, wide, long and high is the love of God for the world, but I'm just so grateful that I've experienced some of it in my own life.

So many people think of God as a strict, hard and often sadistic person who sits in Heaven somewhere just waiting for an opportunity to hit you over the head and smash you down. That is so far from the truth. Someone once asked me in a school lesson, 'What is Hell like?' I replied, 'Can you think of a time when you were very hurt? Can you think of a time when you were really scared and fearful? Then multiply that pain, hurt, fear, etc., by thousands of times and you'll begin to see just a little of what Hell is like.' Similarly, if you can imagine yourself at your most happy, most secure, most joyful and most peaceful and multiply that by thousands of times, then that will give you a little indication of what God in His incredible love has planned for you and me.

I was brought up by my parents to enjoy and experience the love of God and to recognise that Jesus was someone who wanted to be my best friend. God broke into my life very dramatically when I was only six years of age. My parents took me to a Brethren church where every Sunday I heard of how Jesus had died for me.

One day I asked my dad if I could become a Christian. He looked down at his six-year-old daughter and wondered if I really knew what I was doing. I certainly didn't know anything about the Trinity or deep theology, and he explained to me very gently that perhaps I should wait until I was older before making such a big decision. I accepted his advice, but our Father in Heaven thought otherwise.

One Sunday night while Dad was putting my brother to bed and my mum was out at church, I was standing in our lounge, not thinking about Christianity, when I had an amazing experience. I suddenly lost the power in my legs and fell to the floor in front of the couch on my knees. I was confused. What was happening to me? I tried to get up – but couldn't. I was exhausted from trying, so I laid my head down on the couch to gather my strength. After a few seconds I tried to lift my head and found that was impossible also. It was as if a huge hand had been placed over the back of my legs and a huge hand over the back of my neck. Suddenly I realised I was in a praying position. This was the way I had been taught to pray every night by my bed. I knew the Lord was speaking to me and that He wanted me to become a Christian at that point. I didn't know what I should do next, so I said my first ever *real prayer* which was, 'Dear God, I'll tell my daddy.' Immediately the pressure was lifted and I was able to stand.

My father entered the room a few seconds later and I told him exactly what had happened. He then explained to me how to become a Christian and led me step by step through a simple prayer. The joy that flooded my being was quite incredible – I had never been so happy. That night I could hardly sleep as I jumped up and down on my bed in sheer delight and excitement at knowing and experiencing God's love in my life.

The more I've gone on in life the more I've discovered that His love is inexhaustible. I've let Him down many times but He's never let me down. He's always there helping and encouraging me. Sometimes when we're going through a really tough time it's not always easy to see God in it all. Sometimes we *feel* He has left us alone or has turned His back on us – but God never does. I'm constantly amazed by how deceptive our feelings can be.

We must learn to put our faith in the facts (God's word) rather than in our feelings. If we put our faith in our feelings then our spiritual life will go up and down. One morning we wake up feeling good and we *feel* God loves us – the next day we wake up feeling miserable and we *feel* God is nowhere to be seen. God's word says, 'Never will I leave you, never will I forsake you' (Hebrews 13:5). God's word is truth. Which are you going to put your faith in – your feelings or God's word?

As I mentioned in the exercises in chapter 2, I often encourage people to write a psalm when I am leading a spiritual exercise workshop. The initial reactions from people can sometimes be interesting, if not humorous. People begin to relax when they realise that all of us can express ourselves in this way; all you need is a willing and praising heart. You don't have to be a songwriter or poet.

One year when I did this exercise with a group of people in Switzerland, one person wrote a psalm which spoke about 'diving into a sea of God's love'. This psalm delighted us so much that Ray and Robbie (our keyboard player in 65dBA) wrote a song out of it.

SEA OF LOVE
I feel like I'm dreaming
Every time I think of you
I feel I'm in Heaven
Every day
Your love and understanding
In my life
Your loving is eternal
Everything to me.

43

Swimming in the sea of love
In the depth of love
Swimming in the sea of love
Deeper into Him

Waves of love surround me
I can feel your healing touch
Nowhere Lord to run to
Without you
Your heart is like an ocean
All I need
Your arms are always open
Holding on to me.

Robbie Bronnimman, Ray Goudie, Zarc Porter.
Copyright 1994 Integrity/Hosanna! Music/New Generation Music

If you've never experienced God's love or need to experience it much more deeply, then can I encourage you to dive into God's love? He will never let you down. Don't allow hurts and fears from the past to stop you going deeper into His love. (See chapter 7: Dealing with rejection and fear.)

I've counselled many people who have been hurt or abused by others. Some have been hurt deeply by wounding words whilst others have been physically or sexually abused. When you've been crushed by other people, it's often easy to reject all love around, including God's love, in order to protect yourself. This is so understandable, yet you are shutting out the only person who can really help you through the hurt and pain. Quite a number of the young people who have been in our teams have been abused in the past.

One particular girl was physically and sexually abused which left her with deep insecurity. When I first came into contact with her she would hardly look at you. She stared at her feet and was constantly asking for affirmation. It was only as she began to experience God's love for herself that she began to be healed. We asked her to come and live with us, and during the first few months encouraged her to speak out her forgiveness to those who had hurt her. Now, many years later, you would never know she was the same person. Her whole personality blossomed as she began to experience freedom from the hurts and pains she had carried for so long. As she stayed in our home, she began to recognise that God loved her unconditionally and began to experience that love and acceptance for herself more and more.

What an amazing God we have! He never exhausts His love for us – He always has more. We can block Him through sin, unforgiveness or apathy, but despite this, He is always there to forgive us and lead us deeper into Him. After many years of knowing Him, all I can say is I love Him and want to know Him more. It's thrilling to know that God is seeking those who have a passion for Him because He is passionate about us. You only have to look at what He was prepared to do at the cross to begin to discover the depth of His love for you and me. My prayer for you, this week, is that you will not only discover truth about God's love, but that you will experience a fresh touch from God as you dive into the depths of Christ's love.

Verse for the week

'But God demonstrates his own love for us in this: While we were still sinners, Christ died for us' Romans 5:8.

Book of the week

Surprised by the Power of the Spirit, Jack Deere (Kingsway Publications, 1994).

DAY 1

5 mins   Write down your aims for this week. What would you like to see God do in you this week?

10 mins   Read Psalm 146 and write down what you feel God is saying to you.

10 mins   Paraphrase and memorise Psalm 103:11.

5 mins   Spend the remaining time praying – asking God to reveal to you much more of His deep love. Ask Him for revelation this week of how much He loves you.

DAY 2

20 mins   Answer the following questions:

1 What is love?
2 How should love act? See 1 Corinthians 13.
3 Write down ways of expressing love.
4 How would you sense that someone loves you?
5 Be honest, how do you treat those you love?
6 Does it match up to 1 Corinthians 13?
7 Have you ever failed to love someone as you ought? Spend a few minutes asking God to forgive you for the times you have not loved others as you should. Ask Him to help you love righteously.
8 How did God show His love for us? (See 1 John 4:9.)
9 What is the difference between God's standard of love and the world's view of love?

Write down what you can learn from your answers. Also, write down ways in which you can express to God and to others how much you love them. Put those ways into practice in your life.

10 mins   Read Luke 7:36–50. What does God teach us from this passage about love? Write down what you discover.

DAY 3

20 mins   BIBLE STUDY
Read John 1:1–18.

1 Who is the Word?
2 Why did Jesus come to this earth?
3 Read verse 10. Why did the world not recognise who Jesus is?
4 Meditate on verse 12.
5 Paraphrase verse 14.
6 Read verse 16. Write down what blessings you personally have received from God.
7 Read verse 18. Spend a few minutes asking Jesus to make His Father's love more known to you.

10 mins   Go out for a walk with God. Thank Him as you walk for sending Jesus to this earth.

DAY 4

20 mins   Spend a few minutes asking God to help you read the following familiar scripture with new eyes. Ask God to speak to you of His deep love for you through this passage.

Read John 18 and 19:1–37. Write down anything He says to you.

10 mins   Spend the remaining time in worship before God. Thank Him for Jesus and for His incredible love for you. Use various ways to express your worship to God. You will find a list of Biblical ways to worship in the Praise and Worship Workout in chapter 2.

DAY 5

10 mins   Paraphrase Romans 5:6–8.

20 mins   Write out in full the following scriptures:

1 Joel 2:13
2 Romans 5:8

47

3   Romans 8:38 and 39
4   Ephesians 2:4–7
5   1 John 3:1
6   1 John 4:7–9
7   Jeremiah 31:3

Write down what these verses teach us about God's love.

DAY 6

10 mins   Read Psalm 139. Ask God to speak to you about His great love. Write down what you discover.

10 mins   Go out for a walk with God. First of all, thank Him for all the love He has for you and then spend the rest of the time reviewing your memory verse (Psalm 103:11).

10 mins   Read Ephesians 3:16–19. Use Paul's prayer for the Ephesians as the basis for your prayer to God about His love for you, e.g. 'I pray that out of your glorious riches you may strengthen me with power through your Spirit in my inner being,' etc. First of all, write it out, and then read it aloud to God. Make it your prayer for yourself.

DAY 7

10 mins   Ask God for a picture of how He sees you and how much He loves you. You may find God will guide you to a portion of scripture or give you a clear picture in your mind or may whisper something in your ear. Whatever way God speaks, do write down anything you see or hear.

10 mins   Write a psalm to God about His great love.

10 mins   Thank the Lord for all He's done this week to help you realise more of the depth of His love. Acknowledge that we can never fully explore the depths of His love because He loves us so much. Ask Him to continue to help you experience more of His continual, faithful love.

4   Discovering who I am in Christ

One of the biggest surprises that Gideon had in his life was being addressed as a 'mighty warrior' (Judges 6:12). God knew who Gideon was and how in the future he would lead Israel; however, Gideon perceived himself as a weakling rather than a warrior. Here's my paraphrase of verse 15: 'Who am I that you should address me as a warrior? I'm sorry, Lord, you are mistaken this time. Just take a good look at me and my family and you'll know you've made a mistake. A mighty warrior – no way!' You can hear him laugh, can't you? And yet he goes on to trust in God and His word and becomes an incredible man of God whom God uses to destroy the enemy.

One of the biggest surprises of my life is that God should want to use me. After all, who am I that God should use me? Yet as I learned many years ago, it's not our ability that counts, it's our availability. God can take any of us and use us to do incredible things if we remain trusting and obedient to Him. One of my favourite verses is Philippians 4:13 which says, 'I can do everything through him who gives me strength.' We may feel weak or insignificant, but with God's Spirit within us, we can do ALL things.

If you take a look at Joshua 1 you will be amazed at how many times God says to Joshua to be strong and courageous. God knows we need encouragement to discover that in Him we are strong. One of the areas where the enemy can destroy us is telling us that we are weaklings or failures. 'Who do you think you are?' he says. 'Do you imagine for one moment that anything you do will make a difference in this world?' He tries his best to pull us down and often he succeeds because we believe his lies.

At the end of 1994, I attended the Evangelists' Conference in Britain which is administrated by the Evangelical Alliance. I had felt that it was important for me to be there and so I took Shaz Sparks (one of the team members and lead vocalist of 65dBA) with me. During one of the meetings, an announcement was made that they were looking for nominees for the committee that oversaw the conference. Someone I didn't know approached me after the meeting and asked if he could put my name forward. I laughed! I thought he was joking until I suddenly realised he was serious. I told him that if he could get someone to second it, then I would allow him to put my name forward. Immediately, and much to my surprise, one of his friends who was standing beside him said she would second it. So my name went forward as a nominee. I was a little embarrassed because each nominee had to be voted on to the committee by the conference. As I looked around the four hundred evangelists who were there, I realised that not a lot of people knew me. I had been friends with most of the leadership for years; however, I did not know many of the delegates. I committed the whole situation to God in prayer.

At the next meeting, each nominee had to introduce themselves and say a little about their ministry. I went up and spoke for a few minutes, and although I am used to speaking at large events when I got back to my seat the devil was right at my side. As clear as a bell, I heard him say to me, 'Just who do you think you are? Just have a look around the room. Who do you think will vote for you? What ministry do you have anyway? No one's affected for God by your preaching. Do you think your ministry is effective? No way! You're a failure. There's no way God can use you.'

The trouble with the enemy is that he knows how little we think of ourselves and takes a little truth and adds his lies to it. I sat there thinking, 'That's true – who does know me here? There's no way people will vote for me. I shouldn't have allowed my name to go forward in the first place. Yes, you are right – I am a failure. How could I possibly think that anything I do could affect others for God? What ministry have I got anyway?' I could feel myself sinking lower and lower as I began to believe the lies of the enemy. In my desperation, I called out to God to help me. 'Please stop this attack and send me your encouragement, Lord.' I felt so low as I was being bombarded with feelings of failure again and again.

When the meeting finished, a man approached me and said, 'I wanted to come and thank you for all the help you have given my son. He attended a Christian holiday camp where you and the rest of NGM were ministering. He is a completely changed person. He went to the camp lukewarm in his faith and came back red hot. There're two books beside his bed. One is his Bible and the other is your book, and he can't get enough of both of them.' I could hardly talk to the man because tears started to come to my eyes. A few minutes later a woman approached me and thanked me for my ministry as it had meant such a lot to her. On my way out of the meeting, another guy spoke to me and said, 'I'm here because of you.' I asked him what he meant and he told me that when Ray and I and 65dBA were touring the country with the presentation *The Great Awakening*, he had responded to a call to full-time work and was now working in evangelism.

I was overwhelmed at God's grace to me in providing the encouragement I needed just at the right time. However, God doesn't always do that. Sometimes, in circumstances like this, we just have to rebuke the lies of the enemy, and start quoting scripture at him and also to ourselves about who we are in Christ. We are *new* creations – the old has gone – the new has come (2 Corinthians 5:17). So often we listen to the voice of the enemy and believe his lies. We need to start seeing ourselves with the eyes of Jesus. We need to believe what the Bible tells us about ourselves. We are joint heirs with Christ (Romans 8:17). We are part of God's family (John 1:12–13). We have been chosen by God (1 Peter 2:9). I believe that it's important to speak to ourselves and remind ourselves of who we are in Christ.

There's a list of verses in this programme that tell us who we are in Christ. Use them each day or any time Satan tries to deceive you into believing you are a failure. Always remember that God's word is truth, but Satan's native language is lies (John 8:44). The more you reaffirm with scripture who you are in Christ, the easier it will be to accomplish God's destiny for your life. Jesus says in John 8:32, 'You will know the truth, and the truth will set you free.' We need to grab hold of God's truth and believe it. That is one of the reasons why it is so important not only to know your Bible, but also to memorise it and meditate on it.

I left that meeting so encouraged and built up by God and surprise, surprise, I was elected to the Evangelists' Conference planning committee in the end! Let's encourage ourselves by remembering that God sees us as mighty warriors like Gideon. Read the story in Judges 6 and see for yourself how much God used Gideon to fight the enemy and lead a whole nation into victory.

Verse for the week

'I can do everything through him who gives me strength' Philippians 4:13.

Book of the week

Victory over the Darkness, Neil Anderson (Monarch Publications, 1992).

Positive thought for the week

God loves to take ordinary people and do extraordinary things through them.

DAY 1

5 mins   At the beginning of this week, take five minutes to pray and lay down all the preconceived ideas you may have as to who you are in Christ. Ask the Lord to expand your mind this week to understand more of who you are in Christ.

25 mins   Before we can understand who we are in Christ, we need to understand who Christ is. Look up the following verses and write them out in full:

1   John 12:13
2   Romans 6:23
3   Colossians 1:15
4   Hebrews 4:14
5   1 Corinthians 2:8
6   John 3:16
7   John 14:6
8   Luke 1:32
9   John 6:35

Beside each verse write what it tells you about who Christ is.
Spend the rest of the time thanking God for who Jesus Christ is and for all He's done for you.

DAY 2

20 mins   Answer the following questions:

1   Are you a confident person?
2   Do you find it easy/hard to believe in yourself?
3   When you set yourself a task to do, does it get done?
4   Do you feel uncomfortable with success?
5   How do you react to failure?

6 Are you able to receive a compliment from others, or do you immediately put yourself down?

7 If God were to call you to some form of full-time Christian service, how would you feel? Analyse and write down why you respond as you do.

10 mins   Read and meditate on Isaiah 43:18–19. Write down what you receive from God.

DAY 3

30 mins   BIBLE STUDY
Read Ephesians 2.

1 The first three verses tell us what we were like before we came to know God. Write down each phrase that expresses what we were like, e.g. 'dead in your transgressions and sins'.

2 Write down what God has done for us. See verses 4–7 and verses 11–22.

3 Verse 6 says that God has raised us up with Christ. Write down how that makes you feel.

4 Memorise Ephesians 2:8–9.

5 Meditate on verse 10. Write down what you receive from God.

6 Spend the remaining time in prayer, thanking God for your place in Christ. Thank Him for all He's done for you. Base your prayer on verses 4–7 and 11–22.

DAY 4

15 mins   Read Psalm 8. Write down what God says to you through this psalm.

15 mins   Spend this time in energetic praise, thanking God and praising Him for:

1 Who He is.

2 Who you are in Christ.

3 Loving us deeply even though we are formed from dust! Speak out your praises to God.

DAY 5

30 mins   Look up the following scriptures and write down what it says we have and are in Christ:

1 Romans 5:1 – e.g. 'We have been justified through faith, we have peace with God through our Lord Jesus Christ.'
2 Ephesians 1:4
3 Ephesians 1:5
4 Ephesians 1:7
5 Ephesians 1:11
6 Ephesians 2:4–5
7 Ephesians 2:6
8 Ephesians 2:10
9 Colossians 1:22
10 Colossians 2:13–14
11 Colossians 3:3
12 Titus 3:5–7
13 2 Corinthians 5:21

Once you have written each statement, read it aloud. Take time to thank God for each thing He's done for you. Make it your practice to read this list aloud regularly.

DAY 6

10 mins   Go for a walk with God. Memorise Ephesians 3:12 as you walk.

20 mins   Read Hebrews chapter 1 and 2:1–9. James 4:8 says, 'Come near to God and he will come near to you.' Imagine yourself approaching the throne-room of God. How do you feel – confident in Christ? Or unworthy? Look up Hebrews 4:16. Thank the Lord Jesus for giving us access to the Father. Remind yourself that you have access to the Father because of what Jesus has done for you (see Ephesians 2:18). If you still feel unworthy, then rebuke the enemy. Agree with him that in yourself you are unworthy – but speak out that in Christ you have been blessed with every spiritual blessing (see Ephesians 1:3).

Continue to see yourself draw near to your Heavenly Father. Imagine yourself before His throne. Tell him your innermost thoughts. Talk intimately with Him and tell Him you love Him. Hear Him tell you how much He loves you and how special you are to Him. Write down how you feel and anything God says to you.

DAY 7

5 mins   Revise your memory verses – Ephesians 3:12 and Ephesians 2:8–9.

5 mins   Paraphrase 2 Corinthians 5:17.

10 mins   Read and meditate on 2 Timothy 4:8. Write down what God reveals to you through this scripture.

10 mins   Read out your list of positive statements/scriptures again. Write down all you have learned this week. Thank God for His love and goodness to you. Thank Him for who you are in Christ. Ask Him to bring these verses to your mind when the enemy comes to condemn you. Thank Him there is no condemnation in Christ Jesus (Romans 8:1–2).

5 Developing a praising heart

One of the stories in the Old Testament that has meant a lot to me over the years is the story of the battle of Jehoshaphat against Moab and Ammon in 2 Chronicles 20. Here was Jehoshaphat at war against a vast army (see 2 Chronicles 20:2). As you can imagine, he is alarmed and calls all of Judah to fast and seek the Lord. Jehoshaphat knew he could not defeat the enemy on his own, he needed God's help and strength. He knew God was bigger than the enemy. He had a correct picture of God.

Sometimes, our problems seem so big that they overpower us and weigh us down and that's when it's difficult to have a praising heart. I know it's happened to me many times when my problems seem so huge. I've had to pull myself back to focus on God and His word, and when I do, suddenly my picture of God and His amazing strength and power increases and my problems, in the light of a BIG God, seem so small.

We must begin to see God for who He is – a BIG God with incredible power and authority. He is our Heavenly Father who loves us and has our best interests at heart. Take a good look at God and in the light of that picture then take a look at your problem. Jehoshaphat went to his BIG God and sought him for instructions as to how to deal with the problem of this vast army. God speaks and tells him, 'The battle is not yours – it's mine and I will fight it for you' (my paraphrase). Jehoshaphat immediately praises and worships God. His problem was still in front of him – nothing had changed, the enemy was still there – but God had spoken and Jehoshaphat believed Him. The battle was the Lord's, not Jehoshaphat's, and the enemy was no problem for God.

It's so important to hear God's voice in the midst of conflict, because that releases you to praise God through the difficult times. The next day Jehoshaphat sent out the singers at the head of his army to praise God. In the middle of the conflict and the fear, they praised God, and it says in 2 Chronicles 20:22 that 'as they began to sing and praise, the Lord set ambushes against [the enemy] and they were defeated.' They praised their way through the problems. Hallelujah!

There was a time in my life when I had to put this into practice for myself. Some of you may already know that many years ago, Ray went through a real difficult time in his Christian walk. He came to me one day and told me he was giving up Christianity. I was five years married to him at the time, and I looked on him as the spiritual leader in our home. Unknown to me, Ray was living in defeat in his walk with God and he felt he could no longer go on living a life as a hypocrite. He decided the Christian life was not for him.

As you can imagine, I was devastated. I loved Ray with all my heart, yet I had always loved God. I could see if Ray gave up his faith, then we would begin to take separate paths and that could only lead us away from one another. I knew I had a choice to make. I could either give up my relationship with God and go with Ray, thus saving our marriage, or I could trust God for Ray. It was at that moment that I knew although I loved Ray with every fibre of my being, I loved God more. I had always wondered whether I truly did love God more than Ray, but now I was sure of my commitment and feelings. I was determined not to let God go until He had answered me about Ray.

Unknown to Ray, I poured out my heart to God for him. Although I was extremely upset and couldn't stop crying, I wouldn't stop praying until God answered, but unfortunately, it was as if Heaven was closed. The verse that kept going round and round in my mind was Luke 22:31, 'Simon, Simon, Satan has asked to sift you as wheat. But I have prayed for you.' I felt the enemy wanted to destroy Ray so I kept on praying for him.

The whole night and the next day passed without Heaven answering. Around five, that evening, while I was still praying and crying, God finally answered. If He had spoken in an audible voice then I couldn't have heard him more clearly. He said, 'Nancy, don't cry any more. I have heard your prayers and I will answer them. If you could see now what I am going to do in Ray, you just wouldn't believe it. Instead of crying out to me for Ray, praise me for all I'm going to do.' Immediately, I stopped crying. I hadn't heard of people dancing before the Lord, but I certainly danced all around our front room. God had spoken and things were going to be okay.

Ray came back in from work about five minutes later, and in my enthusiasm I told him what God had said. The same cold look that I had seen the night before came back into his eyes as he said, 'Well, if God's going to do that, then He's going to have to do it, as I feel exactly the same as I did last night.' From that moment on, unknown to Ray, I spent time praising God every day for what He was going to do in him, even though I couldn't see it. It was really difficult at times. There were times when I felt angry with God. I remember hitting the pillow one night as I shouted at God, 'Lord, when are you going to fulfil what you have said?' Then I would repent before God, telling Him that I trusted Him to do it in His own time. It was only much later that I realised that from the moment God had spoken, He had begun working behind the scenes, but I didn't realise it. It was only as I praised God every day, that it allowed God to continue to work in the situation. I didn't see even a glimmer of hope until about seven months later and then I could see that God was beginning to do things; however, it was exactly a year later when God broke into Ray's life and began to fulfil all that He had promised me.

It is difficult to praise God through the difficult dark periods of our lives, but as we do so, God will bring His victory into our lives. Not only did God change Ray, but as I spent more time with God every day, my relationship with God also developed and deepened. As it says in 2 Corinthians 4:18, let's 'fix our eyes not on what is seen, but on what is unseen. For what is seen is temporary, but what is unseen is eternal.' Let's develop more of a praising heart. Let's see the enemy routed from our lives through praise!

Verse for the week

'Don't worry about anything; instead, pray about everything ... and don't forget to thank God for his answers' Philippians 4:6 (The Living Bible).

Book of the week

Prison to Praise, Merlin Carothers (Hodder and Stoughton, 1972).

DAY 1

10 mins   Read Psalm 103. Write down what you receive from God through this passage.

10 mins   Write a list of all the things that have happened to you for which you can be thankful to God.

              Go through each situation above in prayer and thank God for His love and care. Ask Him to develop a thankful, praising heart within you this week.

10 mins   Write down every worry and concern in your life right now. Imagine yourself coming into God's throne-room carrying a tray or a sack full of your worries. Lay them down at the feet of Jesus. Give Him each one and see Him pick each one up. Ask Him for His peace. Lose yourself in praise

and worship, thanking God for being in control of all that concerns you. Walk away without the tray/sack, leaving your burdens with Jesus.

DAY 2

30 mins   BIBLE STUDY
Read Philippians chapter 1, then answer the following questions:

1 Who wrote this book?
2 In what circumstances did he write it?
3 What is the main theme of this chapter?
4 What happened when the writer first visited Philippi? (See Acts 16.)
5 What is the writer's relationship like with the church at Philippi? (See verses 3–11.)
6 Read verse 12 – what has happened to him and how has it 'served to advance the gospel'?
7 The writer is obviously in prison for preaching the gospel. Imagine being locked up for years for a crime you didn't commit. Write down how you would imagine your feelings to be.
8 Write down how many times the writer uses the words 'rejoice', 'joy', 'thankfulness' and 'encouraged'.
9 Spend time asking God to develop a praising heart in you.

DAY 3

15 mins   Read Psalm 100. Paraphrase this psalm. Write down what you can learn from what it says.

15 mins   Spend an energetic time of praise before God, thanking Him for who He is, for what He's done for you and for His faithfulness throughout the generations. Using a praise tape may help. You will find a list of Biblical ways to praise in the Praise and Worship Workout in chapter 2.

DAY 4

5 mins   Read and meditate on James 1:2. Write down what you receive from the Lord.

| 5 mins | Memorise James 1:12. |

| 10 mins | Go out for a walk with God. Thank Him for all you see around you. Thank Him for all the blessings He's given you, e.g. your family, home, job, church, etc. During your walk revise your memory verse (James 1:12). |

| 10 mins | Read Psalm 100 again. Write your own psalm of thankfulness to God. |

DAY 5

| 20 mins | Read Matthew 6:25–34. |

1 What does Jesus say we should not do if we are in need?
2 What is Jesus saying is God's heart for you?
3 What should we do if we are in need?
4 Repent of times when you have worried instead of trusting. Ask for forgiveness and for God to remind you of His word each time a worry or concern comes into your mind.
5 Meditate on verse 33. Write down what God says.
6 Memorise verse 33. Write it down on a card and take it with you wherever you go today.

| 10 mins | Read Philippians 4:6–7. Intercede for anything that is concerning you, remembering to follow the instructions in these verses. At the end — ask God to flood you with His peace! |

DAY 6

| 15 mins | Read Psalm 46. Write down what you believe God is saying through this psalm. |

| 15 mins | Go for a walk. As you walk with God, thank Him for all His love and care. Praise Him for who He is and the fact that you are His and He loves you! Also revise your memory verses (James 1:12 and Matthew 6:33). |

DAY 7

20 mins   Answer the following questions:

1   Think through the whole week. Has it been easy/hard to develop a
    praising heart and attitude?
2   Are you normally a positive or negative person? Do you normally look
    for the good or do you normally expect the worst?
3   Analyse and write down how it makes you feel when you are being
    negative.
4   Analyse and write down how it makes you feel when you are positive.
5   Based on your answers above, ask God to make you aware of when
    you are being negative. Spend time asking God to help you have a
    thankful, praising heart.
6   What improvements, if any, have you seen in yourself this week?

10 mins   Spend time praising God. Tell Him you love Him and thank Him for loving
            you. Praise Him for your family and friends. Tell Him you are determined
            that you are going to dwell on the positives, the things that are of good
            report. Write down all the positive things God has done for you this
            week. Praise Him for all the good things He's done for you throughout
            your life.

6   Growing in trust

I suppose if I were to ask you if you had trust in God, your answer would be yes. If we are Christians, then at some point in our life we put our faith and trust in a God we couldn't see but we knew was alive. However, our trust in God should grow and develop as the years go by. It's sometimes easy to trust God when everything is going well, but so much more difficult when there's hardship and problems around. I've found in my experience that God deals with us very gently and takes us gradually through the school of learning to trust in Him, in order to build up our faith in Him. If we learn trust through each experience, then I believe when it comes to bigger situations, our faith has been built to believe God for more.

I remember one of the very first times God taught me to trust Him for finance. We were still living in Scotland at this time, and Ray was in Canada touring with a Christian band. In chapter 12, 'Discovering God's plan for your life', I mention that while Ray was in Canada, God had been doing amazing things with him and totally turned his life around. He phoned me one night to tell me what God had done that evening, totally forgetting about the time difference. He phoned at 11.00 p.m. Canadian time – but of course it was 4.00 a.m. in Scotland! While he was on the phone, he asked if I would bring fifty pounds with me when I went to Canada to see him the following week as his finances had run out.

As Ray had been away for four weeks, he was unaware that finances at home were extremely stretched. I came off the phone and thought, 'Well, Nancy, where are you going to get fifty pounds?' I prayed and asked God to provide it and then remembered that a retired minister in our church had given me ten pounds to take to Ray. The next morning the post arrived and in it was a letter posted in London a couple of days earlier. At that time, we didn't know anyone in London and I wondered who could possibly be writing to us. I opened the letter and inside there was no note, only four ten-pound postal orders made out to Ray and me! I was astonished! I still don't know to this day who posted it, but I am incredibly grateful to God for speaking to someone at the right time. I am really thankful that they were listening and that they responded to God and released the finance that Ray and I needed at that point in time. I dropped to my knees immediately and with tears of joy thanked and praised God for His love and His provision. That was the first time I had to trust God for finance and He made it very easy for me. If He had told me that in the future, Ray and I would be 'living by faith' and totally dependent on Him for finances both for ourselves and for the ministry of NGM, I would have said, 'No way, I don't have the faith for that,' but slowly and surely God has continued to increase our faith and trust in Him.

There have been many situations where we have had to trust God even though it looked as though He was not listening or even paying attention. What do you do when circumstances seem to show that unless God steps in, there's no way out! When Moses led the Israelites out of Egypt, they arrived at the Red Sea to find no way across. When he saw the armies of the Egyptians approaching, he cried out to God to do something! He also had the Israelites moaning and groaning at him, asking, 'Why did you bring us out here to die?' (my paraphrase) (Exodus 14:11–12). Moses did the only thing he could do – pray and trust in God! He had never seen or even heard of God parting a sea before. However, God told him to raise his staff and stretch out his hand over the sea and that He would make a path through the water

66

for the Israelites (Exodus 14:15–16). I'm sure everyone must have thought Moses had gone off his head. Stretching his hand across a sea! What good was that going to do? The armies of Egypt were almost upon them and all he did was to hold his hand across the sea!

We often think miracles in the Bible took place immediately. Sometimes they did, but often it required faith and trust in God's word as people believed what He had said. Moses believed God's word and stood in faith throughout the whole night. He had to keep trusting God throughout the night and eventually God fulfilled His word by parting the Red Sea (Exodus 14:21). As we grow in faith and trust in God, He will expect us to be able to believe His word despite the circumstances around us. Ray and I are still in the school of learning to trust God more. God has still so much to teach us in this area; however, through each testing time, our trust in Him and His great love grows stronger and stronger. He may often test us but He has never let us down.

I remember through one testing time being really confused as to what God was doing. We had been in full-time Christian work for about three years when we felt God tell us to give away what to us was a considerable amount of money. After much prayer, we had told God that we would obey Him even though it meant that we would have nothing to live on unless God provided in some way. A few nights after we had done this, we received a phone call to tell us that our main financial support was going to be cut by ninety per cent to forty pounds per month. I couldn't believe it! What was God doing? How were we going to survive? How were we going to pay the mortgage, never mind eat? Was God trying to tell us something? Perhaps it was no longer right to be in full-time Christian work. To say we spent a rather sleepless night would be an understatement! I was very upset and both of us were incredibly worried. We prayed and asked God to help us understand what was happening to us.

The next morning, we phoned our friends, Ken and Hazel McGreavy, and asked them if we could meet and pray with them. As we travelled to their home in London, we put on a teaching cassette. It was a tape by Floyd McClung of Youth With a Mission. In the tape, he talked about how sometimes when we go 'out on a limb for God' it's as if we look back and see the devil cutting off the branch. However, as we stand firm in God, when the devil finishes cutting off the branch, the tree falls down but the branch remains in the air. In other words, even through tough times, times where it looks like we are cornered and are going to be defeated, God is still in control and He can make the tree fall down and the branch remain in the air. We serve the God of the impossible! We knew this was God's word for us, and as we began to pray we heard God say to us, 'You have asked me many times to increase your faith and that is just what I am doing.' Suddenly, there was a lightness in our spirits. We prayed and asked God to help us trust Him despite the circumstances.

When we arrived in London, we explained to Ken and Hazel what God had already said and we praised God together for the release of peace we had received. Over the next few months, God didn't answer our prayers in the way we had expected. He didn't provide hundreds of pounds for us; instead He sold our home, which had been for sale for nine months, and provided us with a rent-free home for several months. During those months He gradually increased our financial support bit by bit. As it says in 1 Thessalonians 5:24, 'The one who calls you is faithful and he will do it.'

I remember another time when our faith in God was stretched again. We were praying and asking God about our car which we used for school missions. Our car was a rather beaten-up Ford Cortina which kept breaking down. It was really embarrassing. We would arrive at a school where we would do assemblies, classes and a lunch-time concert. When we finished we all piled in the van and the car and headed for our next venue. More often than not, we had to get out of the car and push it to get it started, much to the amusement of the watching school-kids!

During our prayer times, Ray and I felt God tell us that He wanted to give us a brand new car. We were really excited. We shared what we felt God was saying with people we respected in God in order to check that we had heard God right. We began to pray for God to encourage us in our prayers by sending in a few gifts. A number of small gifts started coming in and our faith and trust grew a little more. We prayed and asked God to help us sell our old car as we were about to embark on a national tour with BYFC which would mean our car hardly being used. We could barely contain our excitement when we sold it about a week or two later for the exact amount of money we had asked for. We even told the person who was buying our car all its faults, including the fact that it broke down each time it stopped, but he still wanted it! We felt that selling the car was a real miracle in itself and that encouraged us to believe God for more. Not only that, but some friends phoned us and offered us a loan of a car until we were able to purchase our own. We continued throughout the tour to pray for God's provision for a new car, and the money kept coming in. Then we received a gift of a thousand pounds from a very unexpected source specifically earmarked for our new car.

We then asked God for a business contact who could help us get a good deal. We stayed with some friends, Ian and Marjorie Frith, on the next section of the tour and when we happened to mention that we were praying for someone who could help us get a brand new car for a very good price, they very quickly told us, much to our amazement, that they could help. They had a business deal with a local garage and could arrange to get us a brand new car for a much reduced price. As God was continuing to answer our prayers, we looked into what kind of car we should buy. In the end we picked a Maestro which would cost around five and a half thousand pounds. We already had three thousand five hundred, and so we continued to pray for a further two thousand pounds before ordering it. Another two weeks went by and some more gifts came in but we were still far from the total amount.

Our friend Ian phoned us one day and asked if he should go ahead and order the car. Ray and I prayed and felt a release of faith and trust in our hearts to say 'yes'. We put the phone down and began to panic!! Had we done the right thing? We'd ordered the car, but didn't have enough finance. We decided we could only trust in God for the rest. The day came when Ray had to get on the train at Preston and travel to Birmingham to pick up the car. A few more hundred pounds had come in but not nearly enough to cover the bill.

We prayed and felt Ray should go and collect the car believing that God would somehow step in. While Ray travelled to Birmingham, I was at home having a long conversation with God. I felt God had let us down. Where was the rest of the money? Hadn't He told us to get a new car? I was angry with God and took it out on the carpet I was hoovering at the time. I didn't realise it, but the enemy was undermining God's word again and again. If we look at scripture we will see that this is one of his tactics. In Genesis 3 it tells us that the serpent kept saying to Eve in the Garden of Eden, 'Did God say . . .?'

I eventually sat down and asked God to speak to me. I opened my Bible and it opened at Matthew 19:26 and I read, 'With God all things are possible.' Immediately, I began repenting of my bad attitudes towards God. I apologised for not trusting Him enough and told Him I would continue to trust Him. My Bible had fallen shut. I opened it again and this time it opened at Mark 9:23 and I read, 'Everything is possible for him who believes.' I would never advocate opening your Bible and taking pot luck, as it were, but God made these two verses stand out so boldly that I never saw anything else. I told God I would trust Him to bring His word into being, and suddenly there was a lightness in my spirit. I was able to praise God despite the circumstances and believe Him to work it all out.

While this was going on with me, Ray was travelling by train to Birmingham. He had read these books about people needing finance from God who suddenly met someone on a train or a bus who gave them the exact amount they needed. So, full of anticipation, he boarded his train for Birmingham and sat down and waited for his messenger from God! At the next station, a man got on and sat opposite Ray. He looked at Ray and said, 'Are you a Christian?' Ray thinks to himself, 'This is it!' and starts to imagine pound signs in his eyes before answering with a rather expectant, 'Yes'. The man had noticed Ray's Youth for Christ sticker on his briefcase and chatted away to him for ages about God, before getting off at the next station without giving him a penny! You can imagine how Ray felt at this point. Where was the money? He was getting rather nervous but felt that all he could do was to trust God to somehow work a miracle.

He was met at the station by Ian, who took him to the garage to collect the car. He took out his cheque book to pay, praying that somehow God would enlarge our bank account, when Ian said, 'Oh don't worry about that just yet. You don't have to pay for the car today. I'll send you the invoice in due course.' Relief flooded Ray as he realised God had stepped in.

The more I've gone on with God, the more I have realised that my deadlines are not always the same as God's deadlines. A well-known speaker once said, 'Your faith walk begins when you think it should end.' We thought we had to pay the bill when we collected the car. God knew otherwise. Ray came home with a brand new car and we hadn't needed to pay a penny! When the bill needed paying several months later, God had provided enough money to cover the cost of the car. That incident really taught us to trust God and His word despite the outward circumstances. Ray and I had in our minds that God would work in a certain way and by a certain time, but we learned that

God has many ways in which to meet our needs and that the key is our trust in Him and His faithfulness.

I do pray that as you do this programme God will take you further along the road in your faith walk with Him, whether it be for finance, healing, salvation for friends or family, etc. Do remember, when you are on a faith walk with God, that it is important that you submit what you believe you are receiving from God to others who are mature in the Lord. It not only gives you a safeguard against deception, but also as we grow in trust and faith in God it is important to have people with you who can help you through the difficult times. I pray that your trust in God will grow and develop as God shows you more of Himself day by day.

Verses for the week

'You will keep in perfect peace him whose mind is steadfast, because he trusts in you. Trust in the Lord for ever, for the Lord, the Lord, is the Rock eternal' Isaiah 26:3–4.

Positive thought for the week

Keep growing in trust and walking with God. Dream BIG dreams as there is nothing that you and God cannot accomplish together.

DAY 1

10 mins   Spend the first five minutes telling God of your desire to learn how to trust Him more deeply. Ask Him to teach you this week what it really means to trust and not doubt. Read James 1:2–8. Tell the Lord you want to grow in faith and not be someone who is double-minded and unstable in whatever you do, but someone who has a firm foundation.

10 mins   Read 1 Corinthians 1:4–9. Paraphrase these verses.

10 mins   Go out for a walk with God and memorise 1 Corinthians 1:9 as you walk.
           Write it on a card so that you can take it with you and revise it during
           the day.

DAY 2

25 mins   Jesus encourages us in John 14:1 to 'Trust in God; trust also in me.'

1 What does it mean to trust? Look it up in the dictionary and write down
   the meaning.
2 Write down situations and times in the past when you have trusted in
   God. What did you learn from that experience?
3 Write down situations and times in the past when you haven't trusted
   in God. What did you learn from that experience?
4 Have you ever felt that God has let you down? Why? Explain your
   feelings to God and ask Him for a picture of how He saw that situation. Write down anything that God says to you.
5 Read 1 Thessalonians 5:24. Can you believe this verse to be true for
   you and your circumstances? If not – why not?
6 Spend time asking God for forgiveness for any lack of trust on your
   part in the past. Tell Him you are going to put your confidence and
   trust in Him because 'He is faithful and He will do it'. Thank Him that
   He will never let you down.

5 mins   Revise your memory verse (1 Corinthians 1:9).

DAY 3

30 mins   BIBLE STUDY
           Read Genesis 15, 16, 17 and 21:1–7. This is the story of Abraham and
           Sarah and their faith walk with God.

1 What are you trusting God for at this moment in time?
2 Abraham believed (chapter 15:6) after hearing God's word to Him
   (chapter 15:4–5). It's so important to hear God's word in your

situation. What has God said to you? Ask Him to speak into your situation and let you hear His voice.

3 What was God's promise to Abraham? (Chapter 15.)

4 How did Abraham and Sarah try to work out God's promise? What lessons can we learn from this?

5 Chapter 17. God confirms His word to Abraham again and changes his name. What was the significance of this?

6 Read Romans 4:18–21. Abraham looked at his body and the body of his wife and reckoned they were as good as dead. From a human point of view it seemed impossible for God to do what He had said.

   a) Write down all the human feelings and emotions Abraham must have had.

   b) Can you identify with any of these?

   c) Abraham believed God's word *above* the circumstances. What can we learn from this?

7 How many years did it take for God to fulfil His promise? Spend time praising God that Abraham kept on trusting God even though it was difficult. Ask God to strengthen your faith walk with Him and develop a deeper trust in Him.

It is worth noting that even though Abraham did try and work out God's promise himself rather than waiting on God's timing (i.e. Ishmael – Genesis 16), the Lord glosses over his mistake when it comes to describing Abraham's faith in Romans 4. Therefore, there is no reason for our failures to put us off continuing to learn to trust God.

DAY 4

10 mins   Meditate on Isaiah 26:3–4. Write down anything God says to you through these verses.

10 mins   Ask God how He feels about you. Write down any pictures, visions, feelings or words you may receive.

| 10 mins | Spend time praising God for how He sees you and who He is. Use various ways to express your praise to God. You will find a list of Biblical ways to worship God in the Praise and Worship Workout, chapter 2. |

DAY 5

| 10 mins | Read Psalm 33. Ask God to speak to you through this psalm. Write down anything you hear God saying to you. |

| 20 mins | Look up the following scriptures to discover what happened when people trusted in God. Write down a short account of what happened and what we can learn from each situation. |

1 Daniel 3:8–30
2 2 Kings 18:5–8
3 Daniel 6:1–23

Look up the following scriptures to discover what happened when some people did not trust in God. Write down a short account of what happened and what we can learn from each situation.

1 Numbers 20:12
2 2 Kings 17:13–20

DAY 6

| 5 mins | Revise your memory verse (1 Corinthians 1:9). |

| 10 mins | Read Matthew 6:25–34. Ask God to speak to you through this passage and write down what He says. |

| 15 mins | Go out for a walk with God. Thank Him for the beauty of His creation around you and thank Him for the love and care He took in making it. Thank Him that He knows when a sparrow falls to the ground. Ask Him to expand your mind to help you understand how important you are to Him. |

DAY 7

10 mins   Write a psalm to God on the subject of TRUST.

10 mins   Intercede and pray for friends/family who are going through tough times or who are finding it difficult to trust God. Ask God to give you some scriptures to encourage them. Make sure you give them a note of these scriptures as soon as you can.

10 mins   Write down what you feel you have learned this week on growing in trust with God. Thank God for His faithfulness and love to you personally. Ask Him to help you put into practice what you have been reminded of or learned this week.

7 Dealing with rejection and fear

We all suffer from rejection and fear at some point in our lives, but it's how we deal with them that is important. When we are rejected and hurt, it sometimes makes us want to hide away from others in order to try and protect ourselves; however, this will only allow the hurt to fester and get worse. There are very clear guidelines in scripture about how to deal with hurts and fears. Matthew 6:14–15 tells us that we should forgive those who have hurt us. When we have been hurt really badly, it is often very difficult to forgive the offending person; however, as scripture points out, it is the only way to receive healing ourselves. If we withhold forgiveness to others, then it quite clearly says in Matthew 6:15 that our Heavenly Father will withhold His forgiveness from us. In other words, we end up being in a worse state than we were originally. We can easily get eaten up with bitterness and that in itself can lead to ill health.

Many years ago, a friend of mine was diagnosed as having cancer of the colon. She is a Christian singer and along with her husband sings and preaches in various European countries. Just before they were due to travel to England, she was so ill that the doctors told her that if she made the journey, she would return in a wooden box. They immediately went to prayer and sought to hear from God. They also asked many friends and Christian leaders to pray. They received a letter from a church who had been praying for her which said that if she accepted God's forgiveness then that would release God's healing throughout her body. They also received another letter from a friend in Ireland which said, 'I am the Lord who heals you.' It also said that God wanted to totally heal the cancer and in fact God would give her a brand new colon.

Some years earlier, whilst praying, my friend had felt compelled by God to tell her husband of an incident that happened when she was eighteen. She had befriended a new Christian and in her enthusiasm to help him had naively got involved more intimately that she ought, and as a result ended up becoming pregnant. Her parents were devastated and because of her age and also the disgrace, a decision was made for her to have an abortion. She was told never to tell anyone and the whole situation was completely covered over.

She had lived with her guilty secret for years, and when God asked her to tell her husband, in fear and trembling she confessed her past. The fear that he would divorce her had kept her mouth shut for years. When she finally told her husband, he was sympathetic and totally supportive of her. However, although he had forgiven her, she still hadn't been able to forgive herself. After receiving these letters she knew that God was asking her to do just that. Once she spoke out her forgiveness to herself, her healing started and instead of returning home from England in a coffin, her health had steadily improved.

A couple of years after this, she gave her testimony in public and again, through bringing everything into the open, she felt the healing had been completed. When she went back for a check-up, the doctors were totally amazed to discover that there was not any of the usual scarring in the colon. It was as if she had a completely new colon. God had promised a new colon and complete healing if she would forgive herself. When she did, He kept his promise and the healing was complete. Since then she has not only enjoyed good health, but has also worked extensively for God in Europe for many years. It was only when she released the fear and pain and forgave herself that the Lord was able to heal her. Not all rejection and fear leads to ill health, but in this case it was the ground in my friend's life that allowed the illness to develop.

Many people tell me that they could never forgive those who have hurt them because they don't 'feel' forgiveness. God doesn't ask us to wait until we feel forgiveness before extending forgiveness – He commands us to do it. It is so important to speak out to God your forgiveness towards your abuser. You may not feel forgiveness, but speak it out anyway in sheer obedience to God's word and He will bring your feelings into order in due course.

I've also discovered, when I've been hurt deeply by someone else, that each time the past creeps into my mind, it's important to continue to speak out forgiveness. Many years ago, I was badly hurt by a close friend, but I recognised that unless I forgave her constantly I would end up with bitterness and resentment in my heart. It was only as I continued to forgive and did not allow my mind to dwell on unhelpful thoughts, that I began to feel released from the pain.

The great thing is Jesus can identify one hundred per cent with our hurt and pain. He was rejected so many times in his life. He was rejected by leaders (Mark 8:31); by his family (John 7:5); his friends (Mark 14:50); his disciples (John 6:66) and then by his Heavenly Father who couldn't bear to look on the sin that was placed on His Son (Matthew 27:46). Isaiah 53:3 says, 'He was despised and rejected by men, a man of sorrows, and familiar with suffering.' Yet on the cross He said, 'Father, forgive them, for they do not know what they are doing' (Luke 23:34). If Jesus can forgive those who abused and rejected him, then so can we. It's the way to walk in freedom.

I will be praying that during this week you will discover a deeper revelation of the Father's love and acceptance in your life which will drive out rejection. It's only as we learn how much God loves and accepts us that we will be able to continue to love and accept others. At one point in my life, I remember telling the Lord that I couldn't go on after I had been badly hurt by some friends. I told Him, 'How can I continue to love them when I'm being hurt so badly by them?' God immediately spoke to me and said, 'What if I said that to you every time you hurt me? You have the resources within you to continue to love despite the hurt you feel.' Even though I found it difficult, I discovered His words to be true. May God help you to discover the resources within you to love those who have hurt you.

I would encourage you to dig deep into God's love this week. Ask Him to reveal more of His heart for you. The more I recognise that God loves me and accepts me just as I am, then it releases me to love others more. My prayer for you this week is the same as Paul prayed for the Ephesians in Ephesians 3:17–19, 'I pray that you, being rooted and established in love, may have power, together with all the saints, to grasp how wide and long and high and deep is the love of Christ, and to know this love that surpasses knowledge – that you may be filled to the measure of all the fulness of God.' At some point in the week, you may want to ask a friend or leader you can trust to pray for you. Praying with someone about these things can be very helpful, but do remember we must also learn to walk day by day in God's love and forgiveness.

As well as knowing how to deal with rejection in ourselves, we also need to be careful that we don't reject others by what we do or say. Many years ago we knew a fifteen-year-old boy who through a meeting held in our home became a Christian. His whole life changed completely when he discovered Jesus to be real. He couldn't get enough opportunities of telling others about his best friend. His ambition was to be a preacher like Billy Graham.

He gave his testimony at a young people's meeting and

happened to say that he was now 'open to the Holy Spirit working in his life'. The particular church where he was sharing had, in previous years, gone through a split because of charismatic issues. When the young lad mentioned in his talk that he was 'open to the Spirit', the minister immediately stood up and there and then challenged him as to where in the Bible did it say that you were to be 'open to the Spirit'. He publicly rebuked this young lad and caused him a great deal of hurt and pain, so much so that the 'fire' that had started in him was almost totally snuffed out. This incident caused this young lad to withdraw and stop sharing his testimony in public. We need to be so careful what we say to others. We can damage others so badly by our words.

After one of our meetings at a youth camp, a beautiful young girl came up to us and asked us if we would pray for her as she had a disease called anorexia nervosa. Ray felt he should ask her when it had first started and she told us it had happened when her teacher picked her out in the class and called her 'pear-shaped'. Although, I'm sure, the teacher did not mean any harm by her words, what she said was almost like a curse upon this young girl's life. Since that day, every time she looked at herself in the mirror she saw herself as being pear-shaped and thought she was ugly. She couldn't see for herself that she was a very attractive girl. We prayed and broke the curse of those words over her life and she was immediately healed. She wrote to us a year later to tell us that she had had no problems healthwise since that day.

We grow enormously when we are in an environment of encouragement rather than discouragement. Our son, Daniel, knows he is loved unconditionally by Ray and me, and while he is in our company where he feels secure he will sing at the top of his voice and dance around the room. However, the minute someone else enters the room, the singing and dancing stop. He is free to be himself when he's with us because he knows we love him, but when anyone else enters the room it restricts him because he is no longer in a secure environment. It's just the same for us, isn't it? If we feel secure with others, it releases us to be ourselves. If we feel insecure then it restricts us. Let's determine that we will encourage others around us this week and use our words to build each other up in Christ.

One of the main reasons why we sometimes are afraid of giving ourselves to others is not because we are naturally shy, but usually because we deeply fear that others will reject us. The fear of being hurt, misunderstood, unappreciated or let down keeps many of us from getting involved with others. Instead of being able to give to others, our fear leads us to protect ourselves by holding back in the relationship. We play safe, but we disobey God's command to love others. In John 15:12 Jesus says, 'My command is this: Love each other as I have loved you.' Romans 5:8 also tells us, 'But God demonstrates his own love for us in this: While we were still sinners, Christ died for us.' In other words, He didn't wait until we loved Him before He responded to us in love. He loved us from the beginning even when we didn't love Him. What a challenge to us today.

Fear of man, heights, authority, death, etc., can also restrict our walk with God and cause us to be ineffective in our lives. Many years ago, I knew a lady who was incredibly frightened by the thought of being involved in a nuclear war. She was so driven by her fear that she could hardly talk about anything else. She wouldn't even go on holiday because she didn't want to be away from her family when the war started. She tried to prepare herself for what she felt would be inevitable and because the fear was so real to her, in the end it made her very ill. She couldn't enjoy today because of what tomorrow might bring.

God wants us to be people who are not controlled by fear but trust Him in all areas of our lives. Fear is the enemy of faith and can paralyse our belief in God. As we go through this week, let's analyse what fears, if any, we may have within us and let's ask for a deeper revelation of God's love which drives out all fear (see 1 John 4:18).

┌───┐
│   **Verse for the week**   │
│ 'My command is this: Love each other as I have loved │
│ you' John 15:12.   │
└───┘

┌───┐
│   **Book of the week**   │
│ *Settled Accounts. Learning How to Forgive and Release*, │
│ Joff Day (Sovereign World, 1994).   │
└───┘

DAY 1

5 mins   At the beginning of this week, ask God to draw close to you. Tell Him you want to pull down any barriers to His love you may have within you. Ask Him to reveal, expose and take away any rejection or fears you may have.

5 mins   Look up the word 'anxiety' in the dictionary. Write down its meaning. Look up the word 'trust' in the dictionary and write down its meaning. Which of the two meanings describes how you feel throughout day-to-day life?

10 mins   Read Psalm 34. Write down anything you receive from the Lord through the reading of this psalm.

10 mins   Paraphrase and memorise Philippians 4:6.

DAY 2

30 mins   Answer the following questions:

1 Identify any areas in your life where you may be fearful.
2 Analyse why you are fearful.

3 Do you find it easy/hard to trust God? Why?
4 Do you find it easy/hard to trust others? Why?
5 Do you find it easy/hard to trust your leadership? Why?
6 Is there anyone who has caused you hurt and pain or grief that you have not forgiven?

Look up the following verses and write them out in full:

a) 1 John 1:9
b) Colossians 3:13
c) Luke 6:37
d) Matthew 6:14–15
e) Matthew 18:21–2

What does God say to us through these verses about forgiving others?

God commands us to forgive — even when we don't feel forgiveness. He doesn't want us to wait until we 'feel' forgiveness, He tells us to forgive. Speak out your forgiveness for the people who have hurt you along life's way. Don't worry about your feelings — God will honour your obedience and will bring your feelings into order in time. If you do this in all sincerity it will be a significant time in your spiritual growth.

DAY 3

10 mins   Read Proverbs 3:1–8. Write down anything God says to you.

10 mins   Paraphrase verses 5 and 6.

10 mins   Go for a walk with God. Ask God to fill you with His love and peace. Thank Him that no matter how you feel, the truth is that God loves you with an unconditional love. Continue to speak out your forgiveness to those who have hurt you. Do this any time the hurt comes to mind. Ask God to bless those who have hurt you.

DAY 4

10 mins   Revise your memory verse (Philippians 4:6). Find another verse that carries the same theme as Philippians 4:6. Write it down and paraphrase it.

10 mins   Meditate on Isaiah 12:2–3. Write down what you receive from the Lord. Imagine yourself coming before God in His throne-room. Kneel before Him. Express your love to Him. Thank Him for who He is and for your salvation. Hear Him ask you a few questions:

1 Do you love Jesus?
2 Do you trust Jesus?
3 If your answer was 'yes' to the above, would you still love and trust Him in circumstances that you didn't understand? Have you ever had to do this?

Before you leave His presence, allow His love to enfold you. Look up Jeremiah 31:3 and hear the Lord say to you, 'I have loved you with an everlasting love; I have drawn you with loving-kindness.'

10 mins   Write a psalm to the Lord from the intimacy of your heart for Him.

DAY 5

10 mins   Answer the following questions. Find scripture to back up your answers:

1 Why is Jesus trustworthy?
2 Will Jesus ever let us down?
3 How much does He love us?
4 Does He count us as valuable?

Thank Him for the encouragement these verses bring.

10 mins   Ask God to tell you how much He loves you. Write down what He says or any scripture, pictures, visions you may receive.

10 mins   Express your praise to God. Thank Him for all He means to you. Get excited about your relationship with Jesus. Use dance and other bodily

movements to express your praise. You will find a Biblical list of ways to praise God in the Praise and Worship Workout in chapter 2.

DAY 6

15 mins   Look up the list of fears you noted on the first day. Go through the list and discuss each one with God. Present your fear to God and see Him remove it from you and put it to death! Ask Him to help you trust Him in all circumstances. Thank Him that His perfect love casts out all fear (see 1 John 4:18). Imagine yourself leaving your fears at the cross and walking away with Jesus in total freedom.

15 mins   Read 2 Kings 6:8–23.

1 Elisha's servant was full of fear when he saw the enemy surrounding him and Elisha. What did Elisha do to get rid of his servant's fear?
2 What does this teach us when we are fearful?
3 Read Psalm 91:9–13. Ask God to speak to you through these verses. Write down what God says.
4 Spend some time praying, asking God to forgive you for the times you've been fearful and unaware of His vast army surrounding you. Thank Him for the protection He provides for you every day.

DAY 7

5 mins   Read Ephesians 3:16–19 aloud to God as a personal prayer. Thank Him for the depth of His love for you. Ask Him to help you experience it more and more.

15 mins   BIBLE STUDY
Read John 20:19–31.

1 Write down how the disciples would have felt when Jesus was crucified.
2 Verse 19 says the doors were locked for fear of the Jews. Why were they afraid?
3 Verse 26 tells us that even though they had seen Jesus raised from the

dead, they still had fear in their hearts. What happened to them to give them the boldness to speak out in Acts 2?

4 Confess your fears to the Lord—ask Him to come and fill you with His Holy Spirit. Pray for God to release boldness to you. Also pray for His continued anointing upon your life.

10 mins   Go for a walk with God. Thank Him for all He's done in you this week. Ask Him to remind you of the truths you have learned each time you feel rejected, insecure or fearful. Revise your memory verse as you walk (Philippians 4:6). Also thank and praise Him for the truth of His word.

8   Dealing with disappointment

Disappointment is something we will all experience at some point in our lives. Others will, at times, let us down and fail us even though that may not have been their intention. We may even feel disappointed in ourselves at times. I know I have felt disappointed in myself when I have reacted to a situation in a wrong way. Sometimes, instead of reacting in love, I have responded out of stress and tension and said something I never meant to say. Immediately, disappointment and failure creep in and then the enemy plays on it and it's easy to feel condemned.

Another area that can lead to disappointment is when we've been praying for something and it hasn't happened and we end up feeling disappointed in God. Does He not care? Is He not listening to my prayers? Where were you, God, when I needed you? Many factors can contribute to us feeling disappointed, but it's how we deal with it that matters.

There's a story in the Bible that relates very much to this subject. Mary, Martha and Lazarus were very close to Jesus. They loved Him and valued His friendship very much, yet Mary and Martha must have been so disappointed in Jesus when He delayed His journey to them while their brother, Lazarus, was ill. John 11:3 says that the sisters sent word to Jesus, saying, 'Lord, the one you love is sick.' They were desperate for Jesus to come and lay His hands on their brother, for they knew that if He did, then their brother would not die. Even though they had sent word to Jesus to come quickly, yet it says in verse 6 that He delayed His journey.

Can you imagine how Mary and Martha must have felt? Where is Jesus? What can possibly be keeping Him? Lazarus is going to die. Surely He'll come? They knew that the last time Jesus was in their area, the Jews tried to stone Him, but surely for one of His closest friends, He'll come! Where are you, Lord? Can you imagine how they felt when Lazarus died and Jesus did not even turn up for the funeral? What disappointment must have filled their hearts. Their brother had died and it looked as though Jesus did not even care.

When Jesus eventually arrived Martha went to meet Him and immediately said, 'If you had been here, my brother would not have died.' In other words, 'Where were you? Didn't you get my message?' Mary then went to Jesus and she said the same to Him. It says in verse 32, 'If you had been here, my brother would not have died.' You can just hear her saying, 'Can't you see we needed you?' Even some of the people round about commented, in verse 37, 'Could not he who opened the eyes of the blind man have kept this man from dying?' It was loud and clear. 'Jesus, we are disappointed in you.'

However, Jesus asks for the stone across the tomb to be taken away, and immediately Martha says, 'But, Lord . . . by this time there is a bad odour, for he has been there four days.' Jesus turns to her and says, 'Did I not tell you that if you believed, you would see the glory of God?' In other words, 'Martha, even though you are disappointed, put your faith in me and you will see God's glory.' She obeyed Jesus and gave permission for the stone to be rolled away. When she did, Jesus raised her brother from the dead.

She could have stayed wallowing in her disappointment and allowed it to grow into bitterness against Jesus. Instead she obeyed His instructions and continued to put her faith in God. She didn't understand what was happening, but she trusted Jesus despite the awful circumstances. She did not remain in disappointment, but put her hope and faith in

God, and as she did, it turned her disappointing situation into a victorious one.

Romans 5:5 says, 'And hope [in God] will not disappoint us.' We may feel let down by others many times; however, are we going to allow the disappointments to lead us into bitterness and resentment, thus stopping the glory of God being revealed, or are we going to let it lead us into a deeper faith walk and a greater victory?

It encourages me to look at the life of Job, who even though he had been inflicted with ill health, bereavement, loss of wealth – in fact everything had been taken from him – yet he could say in Job 13:15, 'Though he slay me, yet will I hope in him.' It doesn't matter who we are disappointed in, we need to deal with it by trusting God for the future. We mustn't allow disappointment to lead to bitterness and dryness, but allow disappointment to lead to greater trust and fruitfulness.

In 1987, together with the rest of Heartbeat, we released a single into the secular charts in Britain. We had felt very strongly that God had told us to be a voice through the media for Him. We released a song called 'Tears from Heaven' which got to number thirty-two in the BBC charts and number twenty-one in the independent charts. We were given incredible opportunities through the media to speak out for Jesus. We felt we should release another single and in 1988 we did so. However, this time the Church did not support the single as much as the first, and although this single was voted 'Hit pick of the week' by BBC Radio One we did not get any higher than number seventy. The media people couldn't believe it.

They knew that we had been given incredible support the first time round and had expected that, because 'The Winner' was a better song, this one would break through to the top twenty. Ray had put so much time and effort into this initiative, and when the single was not given enough backing he was really disappointed. It really hit him hard and he felt that he had been let down badly by some of the Christian leaders, especially those that he had regarded as his friends. It was many months later, after carrying his disappointment for so long, that he finally got rid of the hurt he felt. At the Charismatic Leaders' conference, everyone was encouraged to write down their disappointments on a piece of paper, and once they had given them to God to throw them in a rubbish bin, signifying that they were gone for ever. Ray did that, and as he was praying and forgiving those who had disappointed him, Gerald Coates, a good friend of ours who had been very supportive of both releases, came up and prayed for Ray to be released from all the disappointments connected to the release of the single. Ray wept and wept before God as he released all the hurt and pain to Him. Ray felt totally released from the disappointment from that time on.

It's so important to hand over our disappointments to God and to forgive those who have let us down. I'm sure you will find much healing through this simple act. Do remember, if we put our faith and trust in God, He will *never* let us down. Deuteronomy 31:8 says, 'The Lord himself goes before you . . . he will never leave you nor forsake you. Do not be afraid; do not be discouraged.' In Psalm 42, David speaks to his soul and tells his soul to put its trust in God and praise God despite the circumstances. It's so important to speak to our souls and tell them to be lifted up. 'Why are you downcast, O my soul? Why so disturbed within me? Put your hope in God, for I will yet praise him, my Saviour and my God.' We may not understand all God's will or ways, but we do know that He is a God who loves us immensely and constantly works for our good (Romans 8:28).

I am praying that as you work your way through this programme you will discover again for yourself just how committed the Lord is to you, and because of that, you will be refreshed, released and encouraged in Him.

DAY 1

5 mins   Write down your aims for this week. What would you like God to do in you this week?

10 mins   Read Psalm 145. Write down what God says to you. At the end ask the Holy Spirit to come with His healing and refreshment for you.

10 mins   List any areas where you have experienced disappointment in God, others, self, and present them before God in prayer. Tell God you don't fully understand why things like disappointment happen but that you want Him to help you cope with the disappointments we all experience in life.

5 mins   Paraphrase Psalm 145:14–16.

DAY 2

30 mins   BIBLE STUDY
                 Read Genesis 37.

1   Imagine yourself in Joseph's position. How would you have felt when all your brothers hated you and couldn't say a kind word to you? See verse 4.
2   Did Joseph mean any harm to his father or brothers when he related the dream?
3   What did his brothers feel about him? See verse 11.
4   How would Joseph feel at being ill-treated and put down a pit and then sold into slavery?
5   Read Genesis 39. Joseph had a dream from God but everything in his life was going wrong. How did he react? With bitterness? negativism? anger? or did he serve God where he was? See Genesis 39:2–4.

6 In the midst of temptation, how did Joseph react? and why? See verses 6–12.

7 Again his dreams are shattered. Again he is unjustly accused and ill-treated. How would you feel if this happened to you? How did Joseph react?

8 Was the Lord faithful to Joseph?

9 Read Genesis 41. Joseph was eventually made second in command of Egypt. God had fulfilled his dreams. In chapter 42 his brothers bowed down to him. What can we learn from the way Joseph dealt with disappointment?

DAY 3

15 mins   Read Psalm 22. Write down any verses which God highlights. Ask God to speak to you through this chapter and write down what He says to you.

15 mins   Go for a walk with God. Memorise Psalm 22:5 as you walk.

DAY 4

15 mins   Bring a list of disappointments before God. Go through each one and forgive each person who has disappointed you. Read Colossians 3:13; Matthew 6:14–15 and Matthew 18:35. Speak out loud your forgiveness before God. Ask God to forgive you for any bad attitudes you may have had towards them. Throw your list in the rubbish bin after praying as a declaration that you have forgiven and forgotten. Any time you feel disappointment rising again, then forgive them again. Pray for God's blessing to come upon them.

10 mins   Look up the following scriptures and write them out in full.

1 Hebrews 10:22–3
2 Romans 8:28
3 Hebrews 6:10
4 James 4:8a
5 1 Thessalonians 5:24

Ask God to speak to you through these verses and write down beside each one what He says.

5 mins   Answer the following questions:

1 Do you feel loved and accepted by God?
2 Do you feel loved and accepted by close friends?
3 Do you find it easy/hard to trust God? Give reasons.
4 Do you find it easy/hard to trust close friends? Give reasons.

DAY 5

10 mins   List any promises God has given you that have not yet been fulfilled. Ask God if He wants to speak to you about any of these things. Write down what He says.

15 mins   Meditate on 1 Thessalonians 5:24 and 2 Timothy 2:13. Write down what you receive from God through these scriptures.

5 mins   Revise your memory verse (Psalm 22:5).

DAY 6

15 mins   Use your imagination to see yourself coming into God's throne-room. Tell the Lord how much you love Him and ask Him to help you trust Him more. Imagine yourself carrying your disappointments in one hand and God's promises to you in the other. See yourself hand over the disappointments to God. Imagine God taking them together with any bad attitudes you may have had in the past, and throwing them into the deepest sea. Thank Him that they have gone for ever.

Then hand over to the Lord His promises to you. See Him gently take them from you. Thank Him that He is faithful and even if you do not understand all that is happening, you will still trust in Him. Hear Him say that He loves you and hasn't forgotten you. Write down anything else He says.

10 mins   Read Ephesians 1.
Write out and pray Paul's prayer for the Ephesians for yourself: Ephesians

1:17–23 (e.g. 'I keep asking that the God of our Lord Jesus Christ, the glorious Father, may give you the Spirit of wisdom and revelation', etc.).

5 mins   Revise your memory verse (Psalm 22:5).

DAY 7

10 mins   Meditate on Romans 15:13 and write down what you believe God is saying to you.

10 mins   Spend time praising and worshipping God. Thank Him that He is a God who can be trusted and who will never let you down. Ask Him to forgive you for any time when you have allowed circumstances to discourage you. Also ask Him to forgive you for doubting Him and His love. Tell Him that He alone is worthy and that you are glad to be in His family. Use many of the Biblical ways which are listed in the Praise and Worship Workout in chapter 2 to praise Him. Perhaps try singing out a new song of worship to God.

10 mins   Write down all you have learned this week. Go out for a walk with God and thank Him for all He's done in you. Give yourself afresh to Him and tell Him that you will trust Him for the future. Hear Him tell you that no matter what the future holds, He will be with you and He will not forsake you.

9 Dealing with loneliness

I believe that being lonely is one of the most horrible conditions that can happen to you, and know that it is not what God intended for you. Psalm 68:6 says, 'God sets the lonely in families.' God has made us people who need friendship and fellowship, not only with one another but also with Him. The greatest friend we can ever have is God Himself. Proverbs 17:17 says, 'A friend loves at all times' and Proverbs 18:24 says, 'There is a friend who sticks closer than a brother.' God has proved His love for us, not only by what He does for us during our lifetime but also by what He has done for us many years ago on the cross. Jesus gave up everything in order that we might come into a friendship with Him. He is a friend who will never let us down. Hebrews 13:5 says that He will never leave us nor forsake us.

I remember God giving me a word of knowledge at a Christian meeting about someone who was feeling very lonely. God told me that even though she was surrounded by friends, deep inside she was terribly lonely. As I gave this word out that particular evening, a girl a few rows back from the front started to weep with loud cries. I went offstage and went to pray with her. She sobbed as she told me that she had felt exactly the way I had explained it and that she had cried out earlier by herself to God to help her. I explained about God's father's heart for her and how He loved her and understood her loneliness, but that He wanted to change it and replace it with a deep friendship with Him. I prayed for her and as she realised that God wanted to be her friend – her whole face changed. She started to smile, then laugh and dance her way back to her seat.

I believe God not only wants to give us a deeper experience of His love and friendship for us but also wants to release us to have friendships with others around us. We should never feel guilty about needing close relationships with others. Our longing for friendship has been built into us by the One who created us, and is therefore part of His divine design for our lives. We need good relationships with others.

One of the reasons we moved from Malmesbury to Bristol was because Ray and I felt increasingly isolated. All our close friends lived elsewhere and most of them lived in other countries. As the team grew, peer-level friendships became harder. I prayed for years about the longing in my heart to have a friend live near by. When God led us to move from Malmesbury to Bristol, one of the reasons we felt it was right was because of the friendships we had with many people in Bristol Christian Fellowship and in particular with Neil and Zoe Edbrooke, two of the leaders of the church. Through a set of circumstances, not planned by us at all, we have found ourselves living in the same street as Neil and Zoe. God heard my little prayer through the lonely isolated times.

It tells us in 1 Kings 19 about a time when Elijah felt very alone in his work for God. During an intimate time with God, Elijah says, 'The Israelites have rejected your covenant, broken down your altars, and put your prophets to death with the sword. I am the only one left, and now they are trying to kill me too.' You can sense the despondency in his voice. 'Lord, I'm the only one left.' It is really encouraging to note what God does.

First of all, He encourages him to see things correctly. Often, in our loneliness we do not see things as they really are. Tinged with self-pity, hurt and pain it means the way we see things is often incorrect. The Lord encourages Elijah by telling him that he is not the only one left, but in actual fact there are around seven thousand people in Israel who have not bowed the knee to Baal. He gives him a correct perspective of things around him.

The next thing God does is give Elijah a companion – someone to be with him in his ministry. He tells him to go and anoint and train Elisha for future ministry. I believe there is a valuable lesson to be learned here. In friendships we need to learn to *give* as well as take. In order to receive help, care and friendship from Elisha, God was asking Elijah to give of himself to Elisha and train him up for future ministry. When we are lonely, we sometimes wait for others to befriend us, but I believe as we take the initiative and give love, care and friendship to others around us, we will begin to make good friends. It is worth noting that what we *sow* in a relationship is what we will *reap*. We will not develop healthy relationships if we simply seek them for our own needs. In this programme I encourage you to think of ways to bless others around you. If you feel lonely, then try and reach out to others with love and blessing and I'm sure in time you will notice a difference in your relationships.

Another area where God wants us to know we are not alone is in our battle against the evil one. In 2 Kings 6, we are told the story of a time when Elisha and his servant woke up one morning to discover the enemy had surrounded them. Elisha's servant was terrified when he saw the huge army with its many horses and chariots and he cried out to Elisha in fear. Elisha told him not to be afraid, because 'those who are with us are more than those who are with them'. Then Elisha prayed, 'O Lord, open his eyes that he might see [all that you are doing].' The Bible then tells us that the Lord opened the servant's eyes, and he looked and saw the hills full of horses and chariots of fire all round Elisha. When we go through tough times and we feel the enemy is too many for us, just remember this story and ask God to remind you of how many of His forces are with you. Psalm 34:7 tells us that 'the angel of the Lord encamps around those who fear him, and he delivers them'.

If you've been feeling lonely or isolated, then reach out to God this week to show you the depth of His love and friendship for you. Ask Him to deepen your friendship with Him and give you peer-level friendships that will help you and inspire you in your walk with God.

Verse for the week

'I have been crucified with Christ and I no longer live, but Christ lives in me' Galatians 2:20.

Positive thought for the week

I am a new creation; no more in condemnation. The old has gone and the new has come. Hallelujah!

DAY 1

5 mins   Ask God to speak through this week's programme into the emptiness and loneliness you feel. Ask Him to show you this week any areas where you are not seeing things clearly and ask Him to provide for your needs.

10 mins   Answer the following questions:

1 In what areas of your life do you feel lonely?
2 When did your loneliness start?
3 Why do you feel lonely?
4 Have you been hurt by others and has this contributed to your loneliness?
5 Is there anything you could do to change your circumstances so that you are no longer lonely?
6 Is there anyone you can trust, perhaps your church leader or pastor, who could pray with you about how you feel?

| 10 mins | Read John 15. Ask God to speak to you through this chapter about His love for you and write down what you discover. |

| 5 mins | Ask God how He feels about you and write down His reply. |

DAY 2

| 20 mins | Write down all the things you would expect a friend to be to you (loyal, faithful, etc.). Write down all the things you would expect a friend to give you (time, love, etc.). Write down the names of two or three friends or potential friends. Have you given them what you expect from a friendship? |

Write down ways in which you could bless and encourage them and make sure you do so at some point today.

| 10 mins | Meditate on Proverbs 17:17, 'A friend loves at all times.' Write down what you receive from God. |

DAY 3

| 10 mins | Read James 2:23 and Exodus 33:11. It says in these passages that Moses and Abraham were regarded by God as His friends. Spend time telling God you wish to be His friend. Thank Him that He loves you and accepts you. |

| 5 mins | Write down all the things you can think of that God has done for you to show you that He loves you, both from the Bible and also in your own life. |

| 10 mins | Write down ways in which you show your love to God. In view of your opinion of how a friend should give to you, do you feel you have loved God as you should? Spend time asking God for forgiveness for the times you've let Him down, for times when you haven't lived up to your own standards as a friend. |

| 5 mins | Memorise Deuteronomy 31:8. |

DAY 4

30 mins   BIBLE STUDY
Read Ruth 1:1–18.

1 Both Ruth and Naomi were very lonely people. Their husbands had died and there seemed no hope of ever having another husband (see verse 11). How does Naomi cope with her loneliness? (See verse 6.)

2 We can learn from both Ruth and Naomi in their friendship towards one another. Write down what qualities Ruth and Naomi showed each other.

3 Write down how Ruth must feel at losing her husband, giving up her family, country, friends, wealth, etc.

4 How does Ruth cope with the loneliness? (See verse 17.)

5 Write down what you have learned from this passage.

6 It wasn't easy for Ruth or Naomi to cope with the loss of a loved one as well as all the other pressures. I'm sure you are able to identify with their feelings. However, they were determined to put God first, follow Him and trust Him for finance, love, care and also for strength to live up to their commitment to each other and to God. Ask God to give you strength to trust Him in the future for your friendships, finance, love, care and all you need.

DAY 5

15 mins   Paraphrase John 15:12–17.

15 mins   Go for a walk with God. Ask God to forgive you for any self-pity you may have within you. Ask Him to fill you with His love and acceptance. Tell Him of your love for Him. Ask Him to provide friends that would help remove the loneliness. Thank Him for any friends He has already provided.

DAY 6

15 mins   Read John 17. Jesus spent time praying for His friends. Write out a prayer to God for your close friends. Read it aloud to God. Spend time interceding on behalf of your friends.

102

Read Hebrews 7:25. This verse tells us that Jesus is always praying and interceding for us. Isn't it wonderful to know that just as you have been praying for your friends, Jesus has been praying for you. Write down how that makes you feel. Thank the Lord for His incredible love for us.

10 mins   Spend time praising God for your family and friends. Use various ways to express your praise to God. You will find a Biblical list in the Praise and Worship Workout in chapter 2.

5 mins   Review your memory verse (Deuteronomy 31:8).

DAY 7

10 mins   Read Psalm 147. Ask God to speak to you through this psalm and write down what you hear.

10 mins   Thank Him that He understands what it is to be lonely. Read Matthew 26 and 27. Jesus was rejected by His friends (see chapter 26:56), by his family (see John 7:5) and even by His Heavenly Father, who could not bear to look on the sin He had placed on His beloved son (see Matthew 27:46), but Jesus continued through because He loves you and me. Hallelujah!

10 mins   Write down all you have learned this week. Ask God to help you to be a good friend to Him and to others around. Ask Him to continue the work He's started and to remove the loneliness you feel. If you have written down someone's name in answer to question 6 on Day One, then why don't you seek them out and ask them to pray for you. Perhaps share with them all you have learned from this week's programme.

10   Knowing the Holy Spirit

I spent the first twenty-two years of my life going to a Brethren church and although I am very grateful for many of the things I was taught, I was given very little teaching on the Holy Spirit. My parents certainly believed in a supernatural God who was able to heal today and, in fact, my mum often received 'words of knowledge' from God which were incredibly accurate, even though she could never have known the circumstances other than by divine revelation. I grew up in an atmosphere where we expected God to speak to us, but it wasn't until I was in my twenties that God began to show me that I needed to be filled with His Spirit. Ray and I were married by this time and were actively seeking God about full-time Christian work. Clive Calver, who was the National Director of British Youth for Christ, had arranged to come north to our home town of Ayr in Scotland to visit Ray, myself and Sheila Walsh to talk about the possibility of us joining BYFC.

During the day Ray, who was always interested in the theology of the baptism of the Holy Spirit, asked Clive question after question. I have to say although I was interested in what Clive was saying, I never really applied it to me as I thought I had been filled with the Spirit at conversion. Towards the end of the evening, I went to the bathroom and while I was sitting there, minding my own business – God spoke to me! As clear as a bell, I heard God say, 'Ask Clive to pray for you.' I said, 'But why, Lord?' I'm sure God must have thought I was really dumb – I mean, Clive had just spent hours and hours talking about the baptism of the Holy Spirit and here was I, asking God, 'Why?' All God kept saying was, 'Ask Clive to pray for you.' I argued back and forth with God. 'Yes, Lord, I heard you the first time – but please tell me why you want him to pray for me. Clive will immediately ask me, "*What* do you want me to pray for you?" and I will look a real idiot by saying, "I don't know".' However, God just kept on insisting, 'Ask Clive to pray for you.'

After a considerable amount of time had passed, I felt I no longer could remain in the bathroom as I was sure Ray, Sheila and Clive would think I had fallen in! As I walked back into the room, Sheila asked if I could drive her home as it was getting late. When we got in the car, I started to cry. I remember tears pouring down my cheeks as I told Sheila I didn't know why I was crying. I certainly didn't feel like crying, but here I was, in tears. I told her what God had said to me and she encouraged me to ask Clive to pray for me, as she felt he would be delighted to do so. On the way back in the car, I told God if He gave me the opportunity to ask Clive to pray for me then I would do it.

As I arrived home, I looked in the mirror and decided that no one would know I'd been crying. I was wrong! The moment I walked into the room, Clive and Ray immediately asked me, 'What's wrong?' I knew this was God giving me my opportunity, so I blurted out that I believed God wanted me to ask Clive to pray for me. Instead of Clive asking me 'Why?' as I had anticipated, he immediately responded, 'That's great – God told me this afternoon that I had to pray for you.' Clive came over and laid his hands on me and prayed for me to be filled with the Spirit and then prophesied over me. A part of that prophecy, which has remained with me over the years, was that God would give me 'spiritual children' all across the land. I couldn't see at the time how that could come true; however, for many years now, I have been helping, counselling and praying for people who write, phone and visit from all over the UK. Incredible peace and joy filled my whole being and I felt completely different when I went to bed that night.

The next day, during my special time with God, the Holy Spirit began to put strange words in my mouth. I had prayed for a year or two for tongues and nothing had happened – but here I was, speaking a small phrase over and over again. Was this the gift of tongues? Maybe I was just making it up – or perhaps, even worse, maybe it was the devil putting these words in my mouth. After struggling for a while, I began to realise that God only gives good gifts to His children and this really was a special gift from Him. I now know that the enemy often puts doubts in people's minds at the beginning, confusing them as to whether this gift is of God or whether they are making it up themselves. In these circumstances, as someone once said, 'Doubt your doubts.' I have come to discover, over the years, that the gift of tongues is a really special and useful gift which not only builds us up personally but is also essential in prayer and warfare.

There are so many people who are frightened by the Holy Spirit and by the gifts He brings. I'm sure the enemy knows just how essential the Holy Spirit and His gifts are to us, and so he tries his best to frighten us away. Recently, NGM held a national event called 'Shake the Nations' in Bristol. We received many letters afterwards telling us incredible things of what God had done during the programme. One particular person was healed by God, even though no one had prayed for him. Another received the gift of tongues in the middle of the meeting. Many were restored or encouraged in their walk with God. However, amidst all the encouraging letters, we received two where we were told that some young people who came were really scared by the use of tongues in prayer. In fact, one person told Ray on the phone that all this praying in tongues 'scared the hell out of him'. Ray wasn't sure whether to rejoice or sympathise with him! People get frightened for many different reasons: lack of teaching, wrong concepts of God or bad experiences in the past, just to mention a few. Ephesians 5:18 commands us to be filled (and keep on being filled) with the Holy Spirit. You may never have experienced being filled with God's Spirit, or perhaps you already have been filled at some point in your life. However, the question we should be asking ourselves is, 'Are we full of the Spirit now?' I trust as you do this week's programme God will open up more of the Holy Spirit's ministry to you.

Verse for the week

'I baptise you with water for repentance. But after me will come one who is more powerful than I, whose sandals I am not fit to carry. He will baptise you with the Holy Spirit and with fire.' John the Baptist speaking about Jesus in Matthew 3:11.

DAY 1

5 mins   Write down what you are wanting God to do in you this week. Thank God for all He's going to do and say, and ask Him to deeply affect your life.

10 mins   Read Isaiah 40. Write down in full any verses which speak to you and write down what God says.

10 mins   Look up the following scriptures and write down the titles (names) given to the Holy Spirit:

     1   Genesis 1:2
     2   Isaiah 61:1
     3   Matthew 10:20
     4   John 14:17
     5   John 14:26
     6   Romans 1:4
     7   Romans 8:9
     8   Galatians 4:6

9   1 Peter 4:14
10 Psalm 51:11
11 Hebrews 9:14

After reading all these scriptures — would you agree with the statement that the Holy Spirit is God?

5 mins   Thank God for the gift of His Holy Spirit. Ask the Holy Spirit to make Himself known to you in a deeper way during the next few days.

DAY 2

20 mins   We established yesterday that the Holy Spirit is God. Look up the following scriptures to discover a little of what He does. Write down each Holy Spirit activity.

1   Job 33:4
2   Acts 9:31
3   Romans 8:26
4   John 16:8
5   John 14:26
6   Acts 2:4–5
7   1 Corinthians 12:13
8   Romans 15:16
9   Acts 8:29
10 John 16:13
11 1 John 2:20
12 1 Corinthians 12:1–11

10 mins   Go for a walk with the Lord. Look for the Holy Spirit's handiwork in creation around you. Thank Him for His work as you walk. Ask the Lord to reveal more of the Holy Spirit and His work to you.

DAY 3

10 mins   Meditate on John 14:26. Write down what you believe God is saying to you.

20 mins   BIBLE STUDY
Read Luke 11:1–13.

1 Do you have a hunger in your heart to learn how to pray more? Ask God to increase your level of hunger for Him.
2 What is Jesus' main teaching point in verses 5–10?
3 Memorise verses 9 and 10.
4 Paraphrase verses 11–13.
5 Do you have any fear in you when it comes to giving the Holy Spirit control of your life? If so, try and analyse why.
6 According to verse 13, will God ever give you a bad gift?
7 Take a few minutes to ask God to remove any fear from your life and increase your desire to allow His Holy Spirit to have more freedom within you.

DAY 4

10 mins   Look up the following verses and write down what we should be careful not to do to the Holy Spirit.

1 Isaiah 63:10
2 Ephesians 4:30
3 Acts 5:3
4 Psalm 106:33
5 Matthew 12:31

Spend a few minutes telling the Holy Spirit you want to get to know Him better. Ask Him to forgive you for any time you have grieved Him.

20 mins   Read Ezekiel 47. Write down any areas within your life that you know are dead or dry or need God's touch upon them. Put on some meditative music. (I recommend the companion tape to this book — see chapter 1 for details.)

Imagine God's Holy Spirit like a river flowing from Heaven to you. At first it is only a trickle but as you watch and pray and ask God to increase the power, the trickle turns into a stream, then the stream into a small river. The river looks crystal clear — it sparkles in the sun and seems to bring everything around it into life. Encouraged by what you see, you again ask the Holy Spirit to increase His power and authority in your life. At that point ask God to remove any blockages in you to avoid the river being stopped. Confess any sin or areas of darkness (fear, hurt, etc.) you know would be a blockage and ask God to reveal any area that you don't know about that would stop the Holy Spirit flowing freely in your life.

As you confess, begin to see the river increase in depth and width — instead of being a small river, it now turns into a vast deep river which no one could cross. Everything it touches comes alive — dead trees and plants spring back into life.

Ask the Holy Spirit to flood you and fill you and see all the dead/dry areas in your life come alive again. Speak life to your prayer life; your reading of scripture; your witnessing; your good works; your finances; your family; your church; your friends. In your imagination, see it come alive by the touch of the Holy Spirit.

Write down anything God says to you. Thank God for His river of life. Thank Him for filling you full of His Holy Spirit.

DAY 5

5 mins   Ask the Holy Spirit to continue to fill you and indwell you. Again, use your imagination to see that river of His Spirit drench you totally. Commit yourself to going deeper with the Lord.

10 mins   Look up Romans 12:6–8 and 1 Corinthians 12:4–11 and write down the gifts the Holy Spirit brings to us. Ask God to release more of His gifts within your life.

15 mins   Read, paraphrase and write out in full James 1:17. Spend the remaining time thanking and praising God for the Holy Spirit and His gifts. Use bodily movements to praise God — don't restrict your praise to words only. You will find a list of Biblical ways to praise and worship God in the Praise and Worship Workout in chapter 2. You may wish to use a praise tape to help you.

111

DAY 6

20 mins   BIBLE STUDY
          Read Luke 4:1–14.

1. Verse 1 says that Jesus was 'led by the Holy Spirit'. What does this mean and have you seen the Holy Spirit leading you in your life? If so – in what ways?
2. Is it wrong to be tempted by the devil?
3. What was the devil's aim in tempting Jesus?
4. How does Jesus deal with him?
5. Verse 1 says that Jesus was full of the Holy Spirit, and after fasting and seeking God He returned to Galilee in 'the power of the Spirit' (verse 14). Ask God if there's anything He wants you to do to have more of the power of God released in your life. Write down what He says and implement it as soon as possible.

10 mins   Go for a walk with God. Review your memory verses as you walk (Luke 11:9–10).

DAY 7

10 mins   Read Romans 8:1–27. Thank God for the role of the Holy Spirit in your life. Ask God to speak to you through this chapter and write down what you believe God says to you.

10 mins   Write a psalm expressing your appreciation of the work of God in your life.

10 mins   Write down all that you have learned this week and spend time thanking God for all He's done and all He's going to do in and through you.

11　Discovering angels

One of the subjects that is often neglected in Christian teaching is the ministry of angels. I haven't heard too many sermons on angels, although Billy Graham has written a very good instructive book on the subject. Nonetheless, you would have to go through your Bible with your eyes shut to miss the many references there are to angels and their ministry. Angels are mentioned in the Old and New Testaments nearly three hundred times. In the first two chapters of Luke alone, there are three separate occasions where angels appear on the earth. It is interesting to note that around the time of Jesus' birth and the beginning of His earthly ministry there was a lot of angelic activity, and this happened again around the time of His death and resurrection. It is fair to assume, therefore, that this will happen again when there is going to be a significant spiritual happening. It is encouraging to hear of stories of people who have encountered angels in these days.

I recently heard of a lady in America who tells the story of how angels protected her from a rapist. She was driving home late one night, when she heard an announcement over the radio warning people in the area in which she lived that a rapist had escaped from prison and had been seen in the vicinity. They gave a full description of the man and said he was very dangerous. She prayed and asked God to protect her as she travelled home. As she got out of her car, she thought she saw something move in the bushes. She cried out to God again as she hurried down the pathway to her home. As she approached the bushes, she saw the rapist hiding in them and realised that she had to walk right past him. Praying like crazy she walked quickly to her home, got in the front door, and quickly and fearfully phoned the police. She was trembling all over. However, minutes later, the police arrived and promptly arrested the rapist.

She asked the policeman if she could speak to the man and asked him why he did not attack her as she walked past the bush. He immediately said, 'I wasn't going to touch you with those two big guys by your side.' The lady believes that the only explanation is that God sent His angels to protect her. What a comfort to know that God sends His angels to help and protect us.

There was a man in the Bible who was told by Jesus that he would experience an angelic visitation. In John 1:43–51 we read of the conversion of Nathanael who became one of Christ's disciples. He was sitting under a tree one day, when Philip came along and told him that he had found the Messiah. Nathanael is sceptical but he decides to go along anyway and see this 'Messiah' for himself. When Jesus meets Nathanael He speaks as though He knows him, and tells him what He has 'seen' him doing a few minutes earlier, and because of this Nathanael is convinced that this is the Christ. There is no other way that Jesus could know this information other than by divine revelation. Jesus then says to him, 'You believe because I told you I saw you under the fig tree. You shall see greater things than that. I tell you the truth, you shall see Heaven open, and the angels of God ascending and descending on the Son of Man.' What a promise!

Another person in scripture who saw angels ascending and descending from Heaven was Jacob. In Genesis 28:10–17 it tells us that as he was lying asleep, God gave him a very vivid dream. He saw a ladder going from Heaven to earth and the angels were ascending and descending on it. At the top of the ladder, he saw the Lord, who spoke to him and gave him a promise for the future. What an experience!

114

I have never to my knowledge encountered an angel; however, the Bible does tell us that not only do they exist but sometimes they perform their tasks without showing themselves to be angels. Hebrews 13:2 says, 'Do not forget to entertain strangers, for by so doing some people have entertained angels without knowing it.'

One of our team members, Robin Knox, told me a story recently of how he was carried by an angel when he was only a toddler. His family had just moved to a new area in Bristol when Robin's mum, Sheila, was told of a lovely walk by a river. She decided to try this walk on her way home from shopping and remembered that she was told she had to go through a gate to get to the path. However, when she reached there, she discovered that there were two gates. As she walked on, she decided that she must have picked the wrong gate. The pathway became more rough and was less cultivated. It sloped down towards the river and after a while became very difficult to walk. She suddenly became aware that she was in a very dangerous position. Not only did she have her heavy shopping, but she also had Robin, a one-year-old toddler, with her. She tried to go back up the slope, but found she could not. She was fearful of going on in case she and Robin landed in the river. She didn't know what to do.

She cried out to God to help her, and much to her amazement, just at that precise moment, a very big man dressed in fishermen's clothes and boots came up behind her and asked if she needed any help. She told him she was stuck and he immediately lifted Robin and the shopping in his arms. He told her to follow on behind him as he strode confidently along towards safety. Sheila followed as best she could along the side of the river, holding on to branches or anything she could find to keep her from falling.

When she reached the other side, the man made sure she was okay before walking away. She discovered later that it was unusual to see a fisherman beside that particular river. Also, she could not believe how easy it had been to trust this man. She was not in the habit of giving her child to a complete stranger, but she felt she could trust him totally. Was this an angel sent by God to help Sheila and Robin exactly at the time they needed help? Sheila certainly feels this to be the case.

When Ray and I go away from home we never leave without asking God to send His angels to protect our possessions while we are gone. It's wonderful to realise that one of the functions of the angels is to protect us. Psalm 91:11 says, 'He will command his angels concerning you to guard you in all your ways.'

Although we don't normally *see* angels, we can see the result of their help. I remember my mum and dad phoning me a few years back to tell me of an incident which had happened to them. My mum had mislaid her wedding-ring; although she remembered putting it on the dressing-table in her bedroom, when she went to look for it, she couldn't find it anywhere. She and Dad hunted the whole of the bedroom. They took everything off the dressing-table until there was nothing there and then put everything back, bit by bit. They searched everywhere for hours but could not find it. As you can imagine, Mum was upset at the thought of losing her wedding-ring, and before she went to bed that night, she prayed again that God would somehow help her find it.

The next morning, as she was dressing, she noticed the ring sitting in the most prominent place on the dressing-table. Both Mum and Dad know they could not have missed it the day before. It had not been there when they had hunted for it. The only explanation was that God had answered my mum's prayer by sending an angel to find the ring and put it where Mum and Dad would see it.

Although my parents shared that story with me, they hesitated to share it with anyone else in case they would not believe them, until they heard a missionary tell a similar story. She spoke of a time when she had lost some important keys and

116

could not find them anywhere. At a later stage she found them again in a place where she had looked several times. She knew they must have been placed there by an angel, as she had looked at that particular place many times and knew she could not have missed them. It's brilliant to know that God is interested in every area of our lives and sends His angels to help us.

The world has a weird view of angels. Sometimes they are pictured as effeminate weirdos with beautiful wings and bowed heads, usually sitting on a cloud, strumming a harp and wearing a long white nighty, bored out of their minds. The Bible, however, does not picture them like that at all. In Numbers 22:31 the angel of the Lord is pictured as a warrior.

Another myth that the world believes is that angels are humans who have died and gone to Heaven. The Bible tells us quite clearly that angels, like mankind, were created by God. In Colossians 1:16 it tells us that all things, whether 'visible or invisible', were created by God. Hebrews 1:14 calls angels 'ministering spirits' and as such they do not possess physical bodies; however, they often take on physical bodies when God appoints them to special tasks. It is exciting to note that angels have been commissioned to help God's children in their struggles against the enemy. It is interesting to see, in Matthew 26:53, that Jesus tells his disciples as he is arrested that if He prayed to His Father, he could have twelve legions of angels at his disposal. As a legion is six thousand, that means Jesus could have summoned the help of seventy-two thousand angels. He chose not to, because He had you and me in mind. If Jesus had not gone to the cross, then we would have no way of salvation.

It is also important to remember that Satan, although he has great power and is cunning and clever, is not equal to God (John 14:30–1). We must remember that he is only a created angel. He was probably one of the highest-ranking angels in Heaven, if not *the* highest, before his rebellion against God; however, he is not God and never will be. Ezekiel 28:14–17 and Isaiah 14:12–20 tell us a little of what he is really like. He was someone who did not want to serve our God, but in his pride he wanted to become God. When we are under pressure from the enemy we can often forget that Satan is not as powerful as our God. The enemy will always try and deceive us, but do remember that the truth is that our God is much bigger and greater than the enemy, and that the battle against him has already been won on the cross at Calvary. The Bible tells us that at the end of time, Satan and his demons will be condemned to hell (Matthew 25:41).

I pray that as you do this week's programme, you will discover for yourself more about the ministry of angels. We need to be more aware that even though we cannot see them, angelic forces are very real.

Verse for the week

'Praise the Lord, you his angels, you mighty ones who do his bidding, who obey his word' Psalm 103:20.

Book of the week

Angels: God's Secret Agents, Billy Graham (Hodder and Stoughton, 1987).

DAY 1

5 mins — Write down your aims and desires for this week as you go through this programme. Ask God to open your mind as you discover more about the supernatural. Ask God to take from you any preconceived ideas you may have about angels.

10 mins — Read Psalm 91 and write down what you receive from God.

5 mins — Write down your thoughts and perceptions about angels and ask God to confirm over the next few days if these are correct or incorrect.

118

10 mins   Go out for a walk with God and memorise Psalm 91:11–12 as you walk. Thank God for the protection He gives you. Thank Him for the ministry of angels. Ask Him to remind you, even though you cannot see the angelic force, that there are many who are 'with' you.

DAY 2

15 mins   Look up the following scriptures to discover the answers to the following questions:

1 Do angels speak? See Luke 1:19.
2 Are angels to be worshipped? See Revelation 19:10.
3 Do angels marry? See Matthew 22:30.
4 Is it possible for us to have 'guardian angels'? See Matthew 18:10 and Acts 12:15.
5 Is it possible to meet an angel and not know it? See Hebrews 13:2.
6 Are angels sent to serve us? See Hebrews 1:14.
7 What do angels do when someone becomes a Christian? See Luke 15:10.

10 mins   Meditate on Hebrews 1:3. Write down what you receive from this verse.

5 mins   Revise your memory verses (Psalm 91:11–12).

DAY 3

30 mins   BIBLE STUDY
Read Luke 1:5–25.

1 What did it mean to Zechariah to be chosen to go into the temple and burn incense?
2 What was Zechariah's response at seeing an angel?
3 The angel brought good news to Zechariah and his wife, Elizabeth, yet Zechariah met the news with unbelief. What happened to him because of that?
4 How much does unbelief play a part in your own life?

119

Read Luke 1:26–38.

5 What was Mary's response at seeing an angel?
6 She asked questions, as Zechariah had done, but why was she not struck dumb?
7 Imagine and write down how Mary must have felt when she heard the angel's message. She was a young virgin engaged to be married to a man. She must have known that no one would believe her story that she had got pregnant by the Holy Spirit.
8 Meditate on verse 38. Write down what God says to you through this verse.

DAY 4

15 mins Paraphrase Hebrews 2:5–9.

15 mins Spend time thanking God for sending Jesus to die on the cross for us. Thank Him for His salvation plan for our lives. It is interesting to note that there is no salvation plan for angels — once an angel turns away from God, then he is automatically damned. Thank Jesus that He was willing to give up all that He had in Heaven for you. Thank Him that He was willing to be made lower than the angels.

Spend time worshipping Him and thanking Him for your salvation. Use some of the Biblical ways of worship mentioned in the Praise and Worship Workout in chapter 2. Perhaps try some ways that you haven't used before.

DAY 5

10 mins Read Luke 15:1–10. Spend time praying to God about friends or family who do not yet know Him. Ask the Lord if there is anything you can do which would help them come to know Him. Follow any instructions God may give you. Ask the Lord to release His angels to help you do what He has asked you to do.

10 mins Read Revelation 22. Write down what the Lord says to you through the

reading of this chapter. Also, write down what this chapter teaches you about angels and their ministry.

10 mins   Look up the following scriptures to find out how angels helped Jesus in His ministry here on earth. Write your answers down.

    1 Luke 2:10–12
    2 Matthew 4:11
    3 Luke 22:43
    4 Matthew 28:5–7
    5 Acts 1:9–11

DAY 6

10 mins   Read 2 Kings 6:8–23. Write down what you can learn from these verses.

10 mins   Look up the following scriptures to discover what kind of ministry angels have been given in connection with Christians. Write down beside each verse what task angels had to carry out.

    1 Genesis 24:7 and 40
    2 1 Kings 19:5–8
    3 Psalm 34:7
    4 Daniel 6:22
    5 Acts 12:7–10
    6 Matthew 24:31

10 mins   Write a psalm to the Lord thanking Him for all the love and help He gives us day by day.

DAY 7

10 mins   Answer the following questions:

    1 Have you experienced the ministry of angels at any time in the past? If yes, then write down what happened.
    2 If not, then if an angel appeared before you how would you react?

3   Have you been involved at any time in your past with occult or Satanic activity?

4   If yes, then have you renounced Satan and asked someone to pray with you? If your answer is no, then do make sure you see someone in church leadership to talk through what happened to you in the past.

Spend an energetic time praising God for what He means to you. Use new ways of expressing your praise. You will find a list of Biblical ways to praise in the Praise and Worship Workout in chapter 2.

10 mins   Go out for a walk with God. Thank Him for all His love for you and for the way He watches over you and cares for you. Revise your memory verses as you walk. (Psalm 91:11–12.)

10 mins   Go over all your notes for this week. Write down a summary of what you have learned.

12 Discovering God's plan for your life

I've discovered, as I've gone deeper with God, that everything we do in life is training for what lies ahead. I've also discovered that had I known what lay ahead I would have run a mile! In my younger years, I would never have imagined myself to be a preacher, yet here I am spending a lot of my time preaching and teaching in various meetings and celebrations. After all, the first time I was on stage at a Christian event, I fell off it!

It was Unity's first booking in Scotland. Unity was a modern choir initiated by Ray and his brother, Derek, and the first project we embarked upon was a presentation called *Time for Christmas*. I had been asked to do some narration with a friend of mine called Frances. The lights came on us and as she uttered her first word, 'Suddenly . . .', I crossed my legs and discovered that my chair wasn't fully on the stage. Before she could say any more, both I and the chair promptly disappeared from view! The audience thought this was part of the show and fell about laughing.

In my first year with British Youth for Christ, while I was singing with Sheila Walsh, had anyone asked me to say anything publicly that wasn't scripted, you wouldn't have seen me for dust. My mum, like me, had been brought up in a Brethren church and because they did not allow women to speak in church, she was never encouraged to do any public speaking. At a Youth for Christ conference in Scotland, someone asked her to pray publicly. Afterwards, someone took her father aside and told him that his daughter had a real gift in communication from God and should be encouraged to use it. However, because of their Brethren roots, she was never allowed to do so. Although I was brought up in the Brethren church, my mum and dad had the insight to send me for elocution lessons. I was taught how to project my voice and how to speak in public. As time has gone on, I have found this training to be invaluable, and in fact I often use what I learned then to pass on to others, to help them in the art of communication.

One day, while spending quality time with God, I felt that I should list any talents/giftings, however small or inadequate I thought they were, on a piece of paper, and offer them to God as a sacrifice. I remember writing down singing, public speaking (I used to say poetry), typing, etc., and then I presented each one before God. I thanked Him for each gifting but told Him that I voluntarily laid them down and that unless He opened up opportunities for me, I would not push or strive to use them. I didn't feel particularly talented; however, I told Him that if He opened up opportunities, then I would trust Him and take them. I felt I was laying them on God's altar and if He chose to put them to death, then so be it. It reminded me a little of Abraham in Genesis 22 when he was asked to offer Isaac as a burnt offering.

It wasn't until years later that I discovered how important my actions were at that time. Sometimes we trust in our abilities or giftings more than we trust in God, or sometimes our ability to do something becomes more important to us than our relationship with Him. At other times we may feel that our giftings don't amount to very much and feel that God could never use them.

A couple of days later, after laying these things down, I received a phone call from a well-known evangelist, who asked me if I would sing on a national Christian tour called 'Our God Reigns' which would be touring for ten days at all the biggest theatres in the country, starting with three events at the Royal

Albert Hall. I was asked to sing with Dave Pope, Graham Kendrick and Sheila Walsh. It was a real honour to be asked but I didn't feel capable or talented enough to be able to do it. However, because I had told God I would only use my giftings if He opened up the opportunities . . . I gulped hard and said 'Yes'. I'm sure my answer would have been quite different had I not had that special time with God.

When we joined BYFC later, one thing we prayed for was musicians whose first love was God. We wanted people who had 'died' to their music. In other words, music wasn't the most important thing in them – but God was. We wanted them to be professional and dedicated in their art form but the music wasn't to be the most important thing in their lives. When we interview people today for our teams, this is still one of the main things we look for in the volunteers who want to work for God through music. I do believe if you lay down your giftings and trust God to raise them up rather than striving in your own strength to have a place, then God will honour you. I know if you do this, it will be a significant turning point in your life. If you are asking God to confirm whether you should serve Him in full-time Christian work, then again this programme will be very helpful. One of the things God did when he called Ray and me into full-time Christian work was to confirm His call over and over again. Ray was firmly established in his parents' business at the time, and although he had taken five months' leave of absence to drum for Dave Pope in this country and in Canada, he had no intention of ever leaving the business. In fact Ray and I had always said we never wanted to live anywhere else but Scotland. However, we hadn't planned for the voice of God breaking into our lives.

During Ray's time with Dave, several Christian leaders came and asked us if we had ever thought of working full-time for God. We hadn't really given it much thought, but at that time I began to seriously ask God if this could be right for us. One day, I felt

God speak to me and give me an incredible peace in my heart that He was indeed going to lead us into full-time Christian work in the near future. As far as I was concerned, God had spoken, therefore it would definitely happen, but Ray was much more cautious. He wanted to be absolutely sure that this was right. We continued to receive words from scripture that seemed to be pointing us in that direction, but Ray was concerned about his parents' shoe retail business. He didn't want to let his mum and dad down. At that point they wanted to open up another shop and put Ray in charge. How could he possibly tell them that he was thinking of moving away?

While in Canada, Ray attended a large church meeting and at the end, an older man whom he had never met came up and asked him if he felt that God was calling him into full-time work. Ray confirmed that this was so. The man went on to say, 'I felt God ask me to come and speak to you. Many years ago, God called me into full-time work, but because I was involved in my family business and I didn't want to let my parents down, I gave in to family pressure and didn't respond to God's calling. Now, twenty-five years later, I realise I disobeyed God. If this applies to you in any way, do not allow pressures to hold you back from what God wants to do with you.' Ray couldn't believe it, as it described his situation so clearly. Ray knew that God was speaking and that if he didn't do what God had told him to do, he would be living in disobedience.

When we came home from Canada, Clive Calver came up to see us in Ayr about the possibility of us joining British Youth for Christ. While he was with us, we prayed together and Clive gave us a prophecy. One of the things God said through the prophecy was, 'Do not worry about your loved ones, I will look after them – you follow after me.' The scriptures Psalm 37:4–6 were also quoted in the prophecy. Afterwards, Ray turned to me and said, 'Well, if that was God, I'd like Him to confirm that.'

The next morning, a letter arrived from a friend who was in

the merchant navy. The letter had been written several weeks before, but in it he said, 'Ray, I feel I need to stop what I am saying and tell you something I believe God wants you to hear – in fact He may have told you this already.' He went on to quote the prophecy almost word for word and even used the same scriptures. Ray and I were so excited that God had confirmed the prophecy in such a special way. God was confirming over and over again that He wanted us to obey Him and He would look after our loved ones.

We continued to receive confirmation after confirmation through scripture, through others, through our church leadership and through the peace in our hearts. It wasn't easy to obey God. It would have been much easier to have succumbed to pressure to stay in Scotland, but we knew we couldn't disobey God.

It may be that through this programme you will feel the need to resubmit your life to Christ and that, through that decision, God may highlight a new, fresh calling on your life. God may want you to get involved in a particular area of your local church, or get involved more in your local community. It may be a move in your job or to serve Him in some form of mission work at home or abroad. If you feel the Lord may be leading you to a particular area of work for Him, then ask Him to fan it into flame in yourself. If, indeed, it is just your own good idea, then it will fade away; however if it is God, then it will get stronger and stronger in you, as He confirms it again and again. It is important in decisions like this to have your call confirmed by your church leadership. God will often confirm His calling by scripture, through your church leadership, through friends and through the peace in your heart.

Obviously timing is of prime importance. We need to hear God as to when He wants to bring His calling into fruition. We can learn so much from David in the Old Testament where he would not grab his destiny by killing Saul (see 1 Samuel 24). He preferred to wait until God brought His purposes into being. I trust as you seek God for His calling on your life through this programme – whether that means in full-time secular or Christian work – that God will give you clarity and direction for the job that only you can do.

Verse for the week

'Delight yourself in the Lord and he will give you the desires of your heart' Psalm 37:4.

Positive statement for the week

'No eye has seen, no ear has heard, no mind has conceived what God has prepared for those who love him' 1 Corinthians 2:9.

Book of the week

Faith for the Future, Colin Urquhart (Hodder and Stoughton, 1982).

DAY 1

5 mins   Write out your aims for this week. What do you want to achieve? Spend time asking God to do the above.

20 mins BIBLE STUDY
Read John 15.

1 What does Jesus ask us to do in this chapter? List the things He calls us to do.
2 What must we do if we want to bear fruit in and through our lives? (See verses 4 and 5.)
3 Write out every promise in this chapter.
4 Verse 16 says that Jesus chose us – spend a few minutes meditating on the fact that Jesus has chosen you. Write down how it makes you feel.

5 Note in verse 20 what Jesus says about persecution. Write down ways in which you could be persecuted in these days.

6 Spend time asking God to help you to accept persecution as well as blessing both now and in the future.

5 mins   Go out for a short walk with God. Thank Him for creation and the life He has given you. Tell Him you want to live your life for Him.

DAY 2

15 mins   We finished off yesterday thinking about persecution. Read Mark 10:29–30 and Matthew 5:11–12.

1 What type of persecution have you experienced in your life (e.g. people speaking against you because of your faith, etc.)?

2 How do you react when hard times and persecution come along?

3 Find a verse in scripture that tells you how you should react when you are being persecuted.

Spend time asking God to help you rejoice through hardship, pain and misunderstanding.

5 mins   Memorise Matthew 5:11–12.

10 mins   Jesus goes on to say in verse 13 that we are the salt of the earth. Write down all the things that salt does, e.g. cleanses, purifies, etc. Salt is essential for so many things. Jesus is saying that we are essential for His plans and purposes for this world. Write down how that makes you feel. Finish off by thanking God that you are special to Him and His purposes.

DAY 3

30 mins   BIBLE STUDY
Read Genesis 22:1–19.

1 Abraham had prayed for Isaac for many years. God had promised him a son and then in his old age (when he was a hundred years old) Isaac was born. All the promises of God were to be fulfilled through

129

Isaac. Write down how Abraham must have felt when he heard God tell him to sacrifice him as a burnt offering.

2 Isaac was not told that he was going to be the sacrifice – write down how he must have felt when his father bound him and put him on the altar. What can we learn from this?

3 God was pleased with Abraham's obedience and response. What did God say and promise to Abraham (see verses 12 and 15–18)?

4 List what are the most precious things in your life.

5 Paul says in Philippians 3:4–11 that he considers his background (i.e. being a Pharisee, a Hebrew, knowing the law in detail, being intellectual, etc.) rubbish in comparison to knowing Jesus. His background (before he became a Christian) was very special to him. Abraham was willing to sacrifice his beloved son because he trusted God with everything he had. Would you be willing to trust the most precious thing you have to Jesus?

6 If you can, imagine yourself presenting that thing/person to Jesus. As you see Jesus take your 'gift', thank Him that you can trust Him – because He loves you.

DAY 4

20 mins   Write down your natural giftings and talents. Imagine yourself laying each of them at the altar (just as Abraham did with Isaac) before God one by one. Tell God that you voluntarily lay them down and if God never raises them up, then that's all right by you. Tell Him that you will use these giftings if He opens up the way for that to happen. Tell Him that He means more to you than your giftings. Write down anything that God says to you.

10 mins   Go out for a walk with God. Thank Him for who He is and what He means to you. Rejoice that you are in God's family.

DAY 5

10 mins   Put on some quiet meditative music (details of my own tape are in chapter 1) and read Revelation 19:11–16. Use your imagination to see Jesus coming in all His splendour and glory – the King of Kings and Lord of Lords. The rightful King coming to rule and reign.

Imagine Him standing in front of you. Look at His hands and feet. Can you see the nail prints where men cruelly nailed Him to a cross? Look at His back and side and see the marks of a wounded man. A man wounded for you and me as He allowed men to hurt Him and put Him to death on a cross, in order that you and I could have a friendship with our Heavenly Father. Then look into the eyes of Jesus – see the love and compassion He has for you! Hear Him tell you that He loves you.

Imagine yourself picking up a crown and putting it on Jesus' head, and as you do, tell Him that you love Him, and that He is first in your life. Tell Him that you want to follow Him in every way. Tell Him you will go anywhere He tells you to go and you will do anything He tells you to do.

Then imagine Jesus picking up a crown and placing it on your head. Hear Him say to you, 'My child, I love you and I am anointing you – I am commissioning you for all that lies ahead. My word to you is to go into all the world and preach the gospel. Let the world see and hear who I am. Let them know that I live.' At the end write down how you felt and anything God said to you.

10 mins   Read and paraphrase Matthew 28:18–20.

10 mins   Spend time in worship before the King of Kings. Put Him in His rightful place. Thank Him for all that He's done on the cross. Thank Him for all He's done for you and your family. Thank Him for all He's said this morning – then worship and adore Him. You might want to put on an appropriate piece of music. Use body language (kneeling, lying prostrate, bowing, etc.; you will find a Biblical list in the Praise and Worship Workout in chapter 2) to express your worship.

DAY 6

30 mins   Get out a map of your area – or a map of your nation or the world. Ask God what area/nation He would have you pray for. Write down any area/nation God lays on your heart. Collate (now or within the next few days) any information or statistics you can get about this particular place. Pray and intercede for this area/nation. Pray for the advancement of the gospel, for truth and justice to prevail in the following areas:

131

1 Leadership (i.e. king; queen; president; ruler; government; local government, etc.)
2 The people of the land (e.g. children, old people, one-parent families, etc.)
3 The Church (use Paul's prayer in Ephesians 1:16–23)
4 The media
5 Education
6 The business world
7 Politics

Spend at least two or three minutes on each subject. Allow God by His Holy Spirit to pray through you. Read Romans 8:26–7. Express your weakness to pray as you ought and ask the Holy Spirit to help you intercede. Write down anything God says to you.

DAY 7

10 mins   Answer the following questions:

1 Psalm 37:4 says 'Delight yourself in the Lord and he will give you the desires of your heart.' What are the desires of your heart?
2 What is your main aim in life?
3 What, if anything, are you doing practically to outwork your main aim?
4 What would you like to see the Lord do in you? Spend time asking God to fulfil that desire.
5 What specifically do you want the Lord to do through you? Write down your answer and ask God to bring it into reality.
6 Spend a few minutes in silence, then ask God if there is anything He wants to say to you. Write down anything He says.

10 mins   Look through your notes and remind yourself of all God has said to you this week. Thank Him for all He's done in you. Ask Him to help you to be the person He wants you to be. Commit yourself to Him afresh for the future and again tell Him you are willing to go anywhere He tells you to go and do anything He tells you to do.

13   Developing a hunger for God

A question God asked me some time ago was, 'How desperate are you for me to move in your life?' If we are a desperate people who are hungry for God to move in us, then we will be prepared to pray, fast, live in self-denial or do whatever it takes to get closer with God. One of the stories in the Bible that has frequently encouraged me and I have preached about many times is the story of Bartimaeus. In fact, it has inspired us so much that Ray has co-written a song called 'Shout' about this story.

You can imagine the scene, a man sitting by the roadside begging when, all of a sudden, he hears a commotion – the noise level starts to increase all around him. 'What is happening? What's going on?' he asks. 'Oh, don't worry,' he's told, 'It's just Jesus of Nazareth passing by.' His whole being floods with excitement. Jesus of Nazareth! He's the Messiah! If I can just get to him, then my whole life will change. He shouts at the top of his voice. 'Jesus, Son of David, have mercy on me.' Everyone around him tells him to keep quiet. 'Jesus doesn't want to be bothered with the likes of you. Keep the noise down. Just sit there and keep quiet.' Now, at that point, Bartimaeus has a choice. He can sit there and give in to peer pressure, or he can keep going in his desire to get closer to Jesus. What did he do? The Bible tells us that he began to shout even louder. 'Jesus, Son of David, have mercy on me.' Why? Because he was desperate to get to Jesus. He knew if he could only get Jesus' attention then his whole life would change.

How desperate are you for God to move in your life? How hungry are you for God? Are you prepared to ignore the other 'voices' that tell us to stay where we are? There are many voices that will discourage us from going deeper with God, some even from friends or family. Yet, if we want God desperately enough we will be prepared to 'shout' with all our might.

Jesus heard Bartimaeus and called him. He asked him, 'What do you want me to do for you?' It was pretty obvious what Bartimaeus wanted, yet Jesus still asked the question. God knows exactly what your needs are, yet He waits to hear you tell Him. Bartimaeus said, 'Lord, I want to see,' and Jesus replied that his faith had made him well. He got what he wanted.

Another story in the Bible which is similar to this one is the story of the woman with the issue of blood. You can read her story in Luke 8:42–8. Again she was someone who was desperate to get close to Jesus. Wherever Jesus went, crowds would surround Him; however, in this case, the crowd was so vast that it almost crushed Him. It was very difficult for this woman to get to Jesus, but she was determined to get close to Him. So determined that she probably got down on her hands and knees and pushed through the crowd until she could just touch the edge of His cloak. The ground would have been filled with dirt and filth. The roads were not cleaned like they are today. Even though it was common for animals to foul the streets, she did not let that put her off. She was prepared to do anything as long as she got to Jesus. She knew that if she could just touch Him, then her life would never be the same again. Immediately she touched the edge of His cloak, the power of God went through her and she was totally healed. Again, faith was the ingredient that made her well and she got what she wanted.

Another person in scripture who has inspired me with his determination to go deeper with God is Elisha in 2 Kings 2. Elijah and Elisha had been good friends for some time. Elisha had served Elijah faithfully and Elijah had been like a 'father in the Lord' to Elisha. Elisha knew Elijah was about to be taken from him, but he wasn't consumed with insecurity, fear or anxiety about the future, because he was consumed with something else. It says that they were on their way from Gilgal, when Elijah says to Elisha, 'Stay here, the Lord has sent me to Bethel.' In other words, 'You stay here, Elisha – this is a wonderful place to be. You will be fine here. After all, this is the "place of celebration" where the Israelites celebrated the fact that they had put their feet on the promised land. The old had gone and the new was ahead of them. This is a great place to be, Elisha, you stay here, but I'm going on.'

We will always have 'voices' telling us to 'stay here' in our lives. 'Why are you getting so intense about God? Just settle back and be comfortable. It doesn't matter if you don't go deeper with God.' Sometimes, it can be the enemy speaking into our lives, whilst at other times it can be the voice of good and well-meaning friends. Sometimes, however, it can be the voice of God, 'testing' us as to whether we really do want to go on with Him. I believe that it was the Lord's voice here that Elisha heard, testing him as to whether he really did want to go on with Him. What does Elisha say? 'As surely as the Lord lives and you live, I will not leave you.' So Elijah and Elisha went on to Bethel. The same thing happens here. Elijah says to Elisha, 'Stay here, Elisha. The Lord has sent me to Jericho.' Again, you can imagine Elijah saying, 'This is a good place to be, Elisha. Bethel is the "place of intimacy". This is the place where Jacob had his dream and he saw angels ascending and descending on a ladder and at the top he saw the Lord. What a place to be, Elisha! Stay here, this is a wonderful place.' What does Elisha say? 'As surely as the Lord lives and as you live, I will not leave you.' So the two of them walk on to Jericho.

Again, at Jericho the same scene happens again. Elijah says, 'Stay here, Elisha. After all, this is the "place of victory". This is the place where the Israelites fought and won their first battle.

It's an incredible place to be, Elisha. Why don't you stay here?' However, Elisha answers as before. Why was he so determined to go on with Elijah? It was because he was consumed not with insecurity, fear or anxiety at the future, but because he was consumed with having a double portion of Elijah's spirit. In other words, he wanted whatever God had given Elijah. He knew that in order to survive and conquer the future, he needed a double portion of God's Spirit and he was determined to go for it, no matter what the cost. It didn't matter that the road was uncomfortable, long and weary. He was not going to settle back even though these places would have been good places to stop; he knew he wanted more from God.

Elijah asks Elisha the same question that Jesus asked Bartimaeus. 'What do you want me to do for you?' Again, he got what he wanted. It may encourage you to note that the scripture records more miracles happening through Elisha than Elijah. In fact almost double!

What do you want Jesus to do for you? Do you want to go deeper with God? If so, then pursue God with all your strength, and God will give you the desires of your heart (Psalm 37:4). The things that will keep you from pursuing the Lord will be things like tiredness, busyness, lack of appetite for spiritual things, other things – television, etc. – taking up too much of your time. It's important to remember that in the medical world hunger is a sign of returning health and loss of appetite is a sign of sickness. If you have no hunger for God then you can clearly ask yourself, 'What is wrong spiritually?' A new hunger is clearly a healthy sign in the Church today.

I remember Ray telling me that he spoke to a couple of girls after one of our presentations about going deeper with God. They were telling Ray that they didn't have any hunger for God and wondered if there was something wrong with them. Ray asked if they were Christians and if they had been filled with God's Spirit to which they replied 'Yes'. After some discussion,

Ray felt he should ask them if they spent any time alone with God. They said 'No'. They didn't think they needed to spend any time praying, reading the Bible or listening to God. Ray advised them that if they were serious about developing a hunger for God, then they needed to spend time with Him soaking up His word. The facts are that His word and His Spirit fuel our hunger for God.

One of the things I constantly pray for myself is that the hunger I have for God and for His word would increase more and more. My prayer for you as you go through this programme is that God would increase your desire for Him and for His word and also that, through this week, God will meet you in a new, fresh and exciting way.

Verse for the week
'As the deer pants for streams of water, so my soul pants for you, O God' Psalm 42:1.

Book of the week
Passion for Jesus, Mike Bickle (Kingsway Publications, 1994).

DAY 1

5 mins   Write out your aims for this week through this programme. Pray and ask God to open your heart, mind and eyes to receive more from Him.

15 mins   Read Psalm 42. Ask God to speak to you through this psalm and write down what He says. Also, write down any verses which stand out as you read them.

10 mins   Go for a walk with God and memorise Matthew 5:6 as you walk.

DAY 2

30 mins   Answer the following questions:

1 How much time do you normally spend in Bible reading?
2 How much time do you normally spend in prayer?
3 Do you find Bible reading hard? If so, why?
4 Do you find prayer hard? If so, why?
5 Assess if anything practical could be done to help you if you are struggling with prayer and Bible reading.
6 What is your main priority in life?
7 Assess how much time you spend on the following per week:

    a) TV
    b) Reading newspapers/magazines
    c) Eating
    d) Work
    e) Leisure outside the home
    f) Looking after family members
    g) Sleep
    h) Church
    i) God
    j) Any other area

8 Do you feel happy at the way your time is allocated?
9 Pray and ask if God is happy with the way your time is allocated. Write down and implement anything He says.

DAY 3

5 mins   Read Psalm 63:1. Express to God your need of Him. If appropriate, tell Him that you feel dry and want to develop a deep thirsting after Him. Invite Him to do all He wants in your life.

25 mins   BIBLE STUDY
    Read Luke 19:1–10.

    1 Zacchaeus had a deep desire to see Jesus. He was short and because

of the crowds wouldn't be able to see Jesus clearly. What did he do to overcome this difficulty?

2 Take a few minutes to think and write down how Zacchaeus must have felt up that tree, e.g. uncomfortable, etc.

3 Write down how Zacchaeus must have felt when Jesus stopped under the tree and spoke to him and asked to go to his house.

4 What happened to Zacchaeus because of Jesus' touch on his life?

Now answer the following questions:

1 Zacchaeus had a deep desire to see Jesus. How desperate are you to have more of Jesus revealed to you?

2 Zacchaeus was prepared to look a fool up that tree; he was prepared to be uncomfortable. Do you want Jesus desperately enough that you are prepared to be pushed out of your 'comfort' zones?

3 If Jesus was to ask you today, 'What do you want me to do for you?' what would you say?

4 Spend the remaining time asking God to forgive you for any lack of hunger in your life for Him. Ask Him to forgive you for any apathy and ask Him to fuel a deep hunger and thirsting for Him and His word. Pray also that God will change you just the way Zacchaeus was changed.

DAY 4

10 mins   Read Psalm 1. Write down what God says to you through this psalm.

10 mins   Paraphrase Psalm 1:1–3.

10 mins   Go for a walk with God. Thank Him as you walk for the beauty of nature around you. Ask Him to speak to you through nature, e.g. one of the trees. Write down what He says.

DAY 5

30 mins   BIBLE STUDY
Read Genesis 22:1–19.

1 What was Abraham's relationship like with God?
2 Write down how Abraham must have felt when God asked him to sacrifice his one and only son.
3 Why did God ask him to sacrifice Isaac?
4 Write down what characteristics Abraham portrayed in this chapter.

Now answer the following questions:

1 What is your relationship like with God?
2 If God asked you to give up something or someone special to you – what would you do?
3 Is God first in your life? Is there a relationship in your life that comes before God?
4 Spend an honest time in God's presence. If you can, tell Him He's first in your life. Tell Him you want to grow in faith, obedience, righteousness and integrity. Ask Him to help you draw closer to Him.

DAY 6

10 mins   Read John 21:15–19. Write down what you believe God says to you through this scripture.

10 mins   Meditate on Matthew 5:6. Write down what you receive from God through this meditation.

10 mins   Ask God how much He loves you. Write down what He says. Be open to Him giving you a vision or picture.

DAY 7

25 mins   Read John 3:16 and Romans 5:8. Write them out in full and paraphrase them. Answer the following questions:

1 Why did God send His Son to die on a cross?

140

2　What did Jesus give up in order to complete the work His Father gave Him to do?

3　Even though we were enemies of God, Christ still came to save us. What does this say to you about God's love and commitment to you?

4　Jesus gave everything for you — if you can, commit yourself to Him afresh and thank Him again for all His love to you.

5 mins　Spend the remaining time praising God for all you've learned this week. Continue to pray that God would feed your hunger for Him and that nothing and no one would come in between you and your walk with Him.

14 Seeking God for an awakening in your nation

One day in 1985 while Ray was out walking and praying, God spoke to him and said, 'I want you to pray for the nation.' As the ministry team, Heartbeat, we had been praying and interceding for different parts of the nation for many years but had never prayed for the nation as a whole. We decided that we would start meeting regularly in our home to pray together for the nation. We thought that this was something which would be on the sidelines of our ministry – not necessarily central to our vision which was, at that time, 'to be a vehicle for the demonstration of God's power and the reality of His love'. However, after only a few weeks we realised that God was dealing with us in such a way that it was going to be central to our vision.

As we had travelled extensively throughout Britain, we were well aware of the state of our nation. Crime was on the increase, abuse – both physical and sexual – of children was rampant. Old ladies were being mugged, raped and sometimes left for dead. The number of people having abortions had increased and a large percentage of teenagers had slept with someone by the time they had reached sixteen. More and more people were becoming homeless and there was much racial tension. We only had to look in our newspapers to discover that our society was in a dreadful mess.

However, it was only when we asked God the following questions: 'How do you see our nation?' and 'How do you feel about our nation?' that we broke down and wept. God began to give us pictures and visions about how He saw the nation.

One of these pictures was of a huge rubbish tip and the smell going up to God was awful. As we prayed, we began to feel God's anger and hurt at a nation turning its back on Him again and again. We began to wonder how God could put up with this. Yet, in the midst of all the anger and pain that God felt, we also sensed His incredible love and mercy for our land. We began to repent on behalf of the nation – telling God we were sorry for all the horrible things that went on. We asked His forgiveness that we lived in a land that had turned its back on the living God.

After a number of weeks of us praying for the nation in this way, God suddenly changed His spotlight, as it were. Instead of shining it on the nation and highlighting Britain, God began to shine His light into our own hearts and lives. What we saw in our hearts under His spotlight broke us again.

We were a ministry team who were on fire for God yet, under His spotlight, we began to see things like pride, selfishness, greed in our own hearts and lives that seemed a small reflection of what our nation was like. He even challenged us about saying an unkind word to someone and thinking, 'Well, it doesn't matter – I don't need to put that right.' God was putting His finger on things like that and saying, 'It *does* matter, no longer am I prepared to put up with the things that you think don't count.' We began to confess our sins before God and before each other, asking Him to forgive us and cleanse us and make us into the people that He wants us to be.

During one of our half-nights of prayer, when there was a real sense of expectancy, God began to speak powerfully through visions and prophetic words. I saw an incredibly huge tidal wave, coming in towards the shores of our land. As the wave broke it crashed on to England and spread out to encompass the whole of Britain. I also saw it spread out into other nations too. God

144

spoke through this vision and said, 'I am bringing a new wave of my Spirit to this land. Don't look to the old because it will be something new and fresh by my Spirit, and thousands are going to be swept into my Kingdom. I want my people to pray and prepare for all I am about to do, but even if some of my people don't pray or prepare – I am coming anyway.'

What a God we've got. It is not as though we deserve revival, but God in His grace and mercy extends His love towards us. The vision God gave us that evening became central to everything we did. We've since changed our main aim to 'Preparation for Revival'. Everything we do now comes out of the conviction that God is going to pour out His Spirit in these last days in a huge and mighty way. We, as the Church, need to be prepared and ready for all He is going to do.

There was a sense in my heart that preparation needed to be inward as well as outward. God wanted His people to purge out anything that was within them that was not of Him. He also wanted them to have a BIG vision of what He wanted to do. I was reminded that evening of a scene I saw in Spain a few years earlier, while Ray and I were there on holiday.

We were walking along a street, when we noticed a crowd of people trying to get into this church building. As we drew closer we noticed that the church was absolutely full and that many people couldn't get in. We wondered what was going on as you don't usually see churches packed to capacity like that. We got as near as we could and peered into the building to discover that it was just a man at the front, preaching. We don't know what he was saying as he was speaking in Spanish; however, God spoke to me very clearly at that moment. I felt Him saying that the time would come when the churches in Britain would be too small for what He was going to do. There would come a time when churches would be packed and people just wouldn't be able to get in. With all my heart, I said, 'Yes, Lord – do it!'

As the years went by, God began to plant the word 'revival'

on the lips and hearts of people everywhere. I am convinced now more than ever that God is going to pour out His Spirit in a deep way across Britain and many nations of the world. It has been exciting to see and be a part of what God is doing across the world at this particular time. He is pouring out His refreshment on the Church. Incredible signs and wonders are taking place around us. People's lives are being changed as God breaks through. A deeper and more urgent need to pray is coming upon many people. Young and old alike are discovering God in a new way. I believe with all my heart that we have only seen the tip of the iceberg as to what God wants to do. We have been seeing incredible manifestations of God during our team prayer meetings – people laughing, crying, shaking, trembling, moaning, wailing, making all sorts of noises and being drunk in the Spirit, much of it producing a deeper walk and intimacy with Jesus. I don't understand everything God is doing; however, if it's God, and I believe it to be so, then I want everything He has for me.

During our Short-term Teams training in August 1994, as we asked God to come in power, we saw many touched in deep ways. One particular boy was so touched by God, he was staggering around as if he were totally drunk. It reminded me of Acts 2 when the Spirit of God came on the disciples in the upper room. When people saw them they thought they were drunk with wine. Peter stood up and addressed the crowd and said, 'These men are not drunk, as you suppose. It's only nine in the morning!' He went on to explain that what they saw was a mighty outpouring of God's Spirit. This boy was behaving as though he had consumed much alcohol but obviously he hadn't. He was totally drunk in the Spirit.

Eventually, when the meeting had finished, we had to carry him to bed and in the morning we asked him what had been happening. He said he remembered worshipping God and then somehow it was as if God took him to Heaven. Jesus spoke to him and said, 'What do you see?' He said he saw a huge crystal-clear waterfall in Heaven and it was pouring down on the earth. Jesus said to him again, 'What else do you see?' He said he saw a film covering the earth and this film had some holes in it where some of the water was getting through and sprinkling on the land. Then the Lord said to him, 'The day is coming soon when I will remove the film altogether and the earth will receive the full impact of my Spirit.' What a vision from a fifteen-year-old boy! God is certainly on the move.

Our Teams Director, Phil Ball, was so touched by God one night, that he was taken home totally drunk in the Spirit. After he had gone to bed, God told him to get up and look up 1 Kings 17. He started to read and when he got to verse 14 the Lord seemed to highlight this verse: 'For this is what the Lord, the God of Israel, says: "The jar of flour will not be used up and the jug of oil will not run dry until the day the Lord gives rain on the land."'

Edwin Orr, the great theologian, talks of revival as being something that happens to the Church and a great awakening as something that happens to society. We are beginning to see the first fruits of revival, but our hearts long for much more, resulting in a great awakening right across society. I believe that God not only wants to do so much more with us as the Church, but also wants to pour out His Spirit in such a way that an awakening will happen across the nations of the world. Our hearts respond to Him, saying, 'Come, Lord Jesus – do all that's on your heart for this world and pour your Spirit out in deep fresh ways. Let us begin to experience more of your power and grace.'

I do pray as you seek God for a great awakening for your nation that God will pour out His Spirit upon you in new and fresh ways. I know God will use your prayers mightily as you begin to pray and intercede for something that's already on the heart of God.

DAY 1

5 mins   Write down your aims for this week. What would you like to see God do in you and through you during this programme?

10 mins   Read Psalm 36. Write down what God says to you through this passage. Spend time thanking Him for His deep unfailing love for the world.

15 mins   Imagine yourself coming into God's throne-room in Heaven. Ask the following questions about your nation and write down His answers. God will give you pictures and scriptures, etc.

1   How do you feel about my nation, Lord?
2   How do you see my nation?
3   Let me see and feel the love you have for my nation.

DAY 2

5 mins   Based on the scriptures/pictures you received yesterday – spend five minutes interceding for your nation.

15 mins   Answer the following questions:

1   Do you have any friends who are not yet Christians? If so – write down their names. If not – think of ways where you could ask God to develop friendships with those outside the Church.

148

2 Do you regularly pray for them?

3 How often do you pray for your friends at school/college/university/ work?

4 Do you know your neighbours? How often do you pray for them?

Ask God to forgive you for times when you have failed to pray for those around you who don't know Him yet. Commit yourself to pray regularly for them. Write their names on a piece of paper and put it where you will see it every day. Spend even a couple of minutes at some point during the day praying for them. Ask God whether you should fast for them specifically.

10 mins   Go out for a walk with God. Thank Him on your walk for the beauty of the world around you. Thank Him for what He means to you and for the friendship you have with Him. Bring your friends' names before the Lord and pray for ways to present the Lord to them.

DAY 3

10 mins   Go through the following list. All of these things are in your nation. Ask God to reveal if any of the subjects on this list are in your heart and life. Be prepared to allow God who truly sees our hearts to highlight areas that we cannot see.

1 Selfishness

2 Pride

3 Negativity

4 Critical spirit

5 Lacking in love/hardness of heart

6 Bitterness

7 Envy/jealousy

8 Lying (even saying half-truths)

9 Impatience

10 Lacking in kindness

11 Slander (speaking about others behind their backs)

12 Anger

13 Fear
14 Lacking in joy
15 Confusion
16 Rejection (of others, God, self, etc.)
17 Rebellion
18 Lacking in generosity

Tick those you can see are in your life. God may give you some I haven't mentioned; write them down too.

10 mins   Read Isaiah 6:1–8.
Imagine yourself coming before the Lord! Imagine yourself opening the door and going through to the Holy of Holies. See the picture depicted in the first few verses above. Speak out your repentance at any pride, rebellion, etc., that you know is in your life and ask God to cleanse you and forgive you. Ask God to forgive you for any of the things you have ticked above. Acknowledge before God that your righteousness comes from Christ and from all that He did on the cross for you. Thank Him for His forgiveness and for His deep love for you. Ask God if there is anything He wants to say to you and write down what you receive from Him while you are in His holy presence.

10 mins   Memorise 2 Corinthians 5:17. Spend time thanking God for the encouragement this verse brings. Thank God for the newness of life given to us through the cross. Ask Him to fill you with His Holy Spirit.

DAY 4

10 mins   Read and meditate on Philippians 1:3–6. Write down anything God says through this meditation.

10 mins   Read Philippians 1:9. This is Paul's prayer for the Philippians. Pray this prayer for yourself and also for the Church in your area and in the nation.

10 mins   Paraphrase Colossians 2:13–15.

DAY 5

15 mins   Ask God how He feels about the following in your nation:

1   Child abuse (physical and sexual)
2   Treatment of old people
3   The homeless
4   Abortions
5   Violence (murder, rape, etc.)

Spend two or three minutes on each one. Write down what God says to you.

15 mins   Spend time praying about these five areas and any more God may add. Allow the Holy Spirit to intercede with tears, groans, wails, etc., through you.

After you have finished, thank God that even though evil is so strong, Jesus is stronger, and with His help we can make a difference in our land.

DAY 6

10 mins   Go for a walk with God. Ask God for a picture of how He sees you. Thank Him for His love for you. Thank God as you walk for His Church in your nation. Thank Him for the army He's raising up to fight the enemy. Thank Him for all the positive things He's doing at this time.

20 mins   Read Ezekiel 37:1–14.

Put on some meditative music (again, my own tape may help here, see chapter 1 for details). Close your eyes and picture the valley that you have just read about. Imagine all the bones lying around. Dead, dry bones. Death and destruction lie all around. It feels cold and empty.

Now think of situations around you that look impossible or have the touch of death upon them. Perhaps you have been praying for a family member or friend to become a Christian but so far nothing has happened. Perhaps you've been praying for a friend to be healed but again nothing has happened. Whatever it is, I want you to imagine them as those dead and dry bones.

151

Imagine Jesus standing with you looking at this valley. Hear Him say to you, 'Can these bones live?' You respond as Ezekiel did, 'Oh Lord, only you know. This situation seems impossible for me, but I do believe you are the God of the impossible.' Then the Lord turns and says to you, 'I want you to prophesy to the bones, prophesy to your situations and speak the word of God into them.'

Speak 'words of life' into them. 'Dry bones, hear the word of the Lord – I speak to you in the name of the living God and I speak the life of God into you.' As you do so, listen for the rattling of the bones as they come together. Look and see the bones and tendons coming together and flesh appearing. See God begin to touch that particular situation.

Then the Lord speaks again. 'Now prophesy to the breath and see the Spirit of God fall upon these people.' As you prophesy the breath and life of God into your situation, begin to see God bring His life to them. Instead of dead, dry bones lying on the valley floor, begin to see a vast, living army. Begin to see your situation come to life in God.

Thank God for His power and love. Thank Him for all He's going to do in your situation. Thank Him for all you saw as He took you to the Valley of dry bones. Pray and intercede for it to become reality in your life.

DAY 7

10 mins   Read and meditate on Luke 10:2. Write down what God says.

10 mins   Write a psalm to God about your nation and your desires for it.

10 mins   Thank God for all He's said this week. Pray for a greater love in your heart for your nation and for those around you who aren't yet Christians. Pray for a great awakening to flood and drench the land. Use the lyrics of the following song to pray to God for an awakening for your nation. Thank God for His incredible love for you and your nation. Thank Him for all He's doing and all He's going to do.

GREAT AWAKENING

Lord, pour out your Spirit
On all the peoples of the earth.
Let your sons and daughters
Speak your words of prophecy.
Send us dreams and visions
Reveal the secrets of your heart.
Lord, our faith is rising
Let all Heaven sound the coming of your day.

There's gonna be a great awakening
There's gonna be a great revival in our land
There's gonna be a great awakening
And everyone who calls on Jesus they will be saved.

Lord, pour out your Spirit
On all the nations of the world.
Let them see your glory
Let them fall in reverent awe.
Show your mighty power
Shake the heavens and the earth.
Lord, the world is waiting
Let creation see the coming of your day.

Ray Goudie, Dave Bankhead, Steve Bassett.
Copyright 1993 Integrity/Hosanna! Music/New Generation Music

15 Growing in intercession

While Ray, myself and one of our teams were ministering in the States in June 1994, we had the privilege of visiting and taking part in *Rock the Nations*, an event organised by the Kansas City Fellowship. As a ministry we have been involved in intercession for years, yet I was blown away by the depth of intercession I saw at this conference. People were on their knees, lying prostrate before God, crying out with loud wailings and deep groans as they interceded for the nations of the world. This had not been instigated from the platform, but people out of their own desire to pray and intercede began to go to the ministry room after the main meeting was finished in order to pray. The most exciting thing for me was that the people interceding were in their teens or early twenties. It has given me a fresh vision to pray and ask God to continue to raise up an army of intercessors across this nation and indeed across the world.

People often think that prayer is boring, but nothing can be further from the truth. It can be hard work but not boring. That's not to say I haven't been to some pretty boring prayer meetings in my time! Real prayer is exciting. As I said in my first book, *Developing Spiritual Wholeness*, prayer is not a one-way conversation, but prayer is a two-way conversation. In other words, we speak to God and God speaks to us. What could be more exciting than communicating with the most powerful being in existence? Circumstances and situations can be altered through praying to God. I've seen it happen so many times.

Some time ago, we were looking for a school in which to hold our Short-term Teams training. We eventually found a school which would be ideal but we were unable, because of our diary commitments, to confirm the booking at that time. We had been told the school was not booked at this point; however, we would need to proceed quickly as another person might want to book it. A few weeks later when we went back to confirm it, we discovered it was no longer available. We were so disappointed. What should we do? Should we look elsewhere? We took the problem to God in prayer and we felt God confirm that He had given us this place and that it was the right building for us. It was important for us to hear what God was saying in this situation because, without Him stepping in, we would have had to accept the circumstances as they were. However, in this instance it was so clear that God had spoken and that He was asking us to trust Him.

We went back to the school and asked if there was any way the person who had booked the week we wanted would change his dates to help us. The school told us that they would not be prepared to ask and that they were sorry but there was nothing they could do. Ray phoned back again and this time we were told that perhaps we could share the building with the other group who had booked the school. The school said they would get back to us after the weekend. We kept praying. We knew we couldn't share the building, so we were still looking for a miracle. A few days later, we got a phone call saying that we could have the whole building to ourselves. God had stepped in. As we prayed and exercised our faith, God answered our prayers and made the impossible possible.

Someone once explained prayer like this. When we pray it's as if we are giving God bullets for His gun, to enable Him to shoot down the enemy. God uses our prayers to bring His purposes and plans into existence. It's so exciting to be working with a God who is not restricted by human limitations. As it says in Matthew 19:26, 'with God all things are possible'.

We have often explained in our seminars that an intercessor is someone who is willing to 'stand in the gap' and take a hold of God with one hand and the person or situation that you are interceding for in the other hand, and bring the two together. As it says in Ezekiel 22:30, God is looking for someone to stand in the gap on behalf of the people. God is looking for those who will be willing to intercede. I know that if we fully understood what could be accomplished through prayer, we would go for it with all our hearts. The enemy knows how powerful prayer is and will stop us at all costs from praying. He distracts us away from prayer and tells us that our prayers are ineffective, but this could not be further from the truth. Every prayer, no matter how brief or simple, is a powerful weapon in God's hands.

I remember many years ago when Ray and I were visiting South Africa, God woke us up in the middle of the night and asked us to pray. We began to pray and intercede for peace for the nations. We assumed since we were in South Africa that God was asking us to pray for peace in that nation; however, we felt we should pray generally for peace throughout the world. We knew that God was speaking to us about strife and war and that it was urgent for His people to intercede for peace. We felt that there was a battle raging in the unseen realm against the heavenly forces and that God was calling His people to pray. We were reminded as we prayed and interceded that it says in Ephesians 6:12, 'Our struggle is not against flesh and blood, but against the rulers, against the authorities, against the powers of this dark world and against the spiritual forces of evil in the heavenly realms.'

The next morning, we heard on the news that America had sent planes to bomb Libya and that complications and tensions had arisen from that decision. We also heard throughout the coming months that God had woken many people in the middle of the night and urged them to pray. God uses our intercession if we are open, available and listening to Him.

One area we all struggle with is our flesh life, which rebels against getting up early to pray, etc. It's in those times that we need to be exercising spiritually – ignoring the voice of our flesh life which tells us to take it easy – and to discipline ourselves to spend time talking and listening to God.

I don't believe that anyone finds prayer easy, but its rewards are enormous, not only for ourselves but for those for whom we are praying. Somehow, when we are desperate for God to move in a particular situation, prayer suddenly becomes easier – but let's not wait until we are 'desperate', let's find out what it is like to become a prayer warrior for God. Let's stir ourselves into action this week. Let's allow God to intercede through us and discover how God can use us to affect many situations, not only in our area but right across the world. Never forget we are in a battle, and one of the most powerful weapons we have is prayer.

Verse for the week

'Pray in the Spirit on all occasions with all kinds of prayers and requests. With this in mind, be alert and always keep on praying for all the saints' Ephesians 6:18.

Book of the week

Prayer: Key to Revival, Paul Y. Cho (Word Books, 1985).

DAY 1

5 mins   Read Luke 11:1. Spend a few minutes asking God to teach you how to pray and intercede.

10 mins   Look up Hebrews 7:25 and Romans 8:34 and Romans 8:26. Remind yourself from these verses that Jesus Himself is the great intercessor who is constantly interceding for us before the throne of God. What

an amazing truth – that Jesus is interceding for us right now. Also, that when we don't know how to pray the Holy Spirit intercedes on our behalf before God. Take time to thank the Holy Spirit for helping you in your intercession. Also thank Jesus for His constant prayers for you. As Jesus is the greatest intercessor who ever lived, ask Him to teach you how to pray and intercede more effectively.

10 mins   Read Luke 11:1–13. Write down what God says to you.

5 mins   Memorise Luke 11:9–10.

DAY 2

10 mins   Look up the following scriptures and write down the reasons why prayers are sometimes not answered:

1 Psalm 66:18
2 James 4:3
3 Proverbs 21:13
4 Luke 18:9–14

Go through each reason and if you can see any of these things in your life, then ask God to forgive you. Accept God's forgiveness and thank Him that He wants to answer our prayers. Thank Him that He has a plan and purpose for your life and wants to use you to pray for others more effectively. Ask Him to teach you more about prayer.

15 mins   Write down what would hinder you from praying, e.g. lack of time, etc. Take time to go through each hindrance and ask God to give you answers to overcome these problems. For example – lack of time – look at your priorities and reschedule your diary or get up earlier to get everything accomplished. Again, ask God to help you to pray and not have your mind and energies diverted to other things.

5 mins   Revise your memory verses (Luke 11:9–10).

DAY 3

30 mins   Read John 17. Jesus prays for Himself, His special friends the disciples and then all believers. Write out a prayer to God for the following and then read the prayers aloud to God:

1 Yourself
2 Friends and family
3 Your church
4 The Church worldwide

DAY 4

25 mins   Write out a list of people or situations for which you would like to intercede. Take each subject and intercede for a few minutes each. Write down any scriptures or words God gives you. If you use the gift of tongues, then intercede in tongues for a few minutes for each subject. Perhaps use your imagination to see circumstances change through your prayers (see the Meditation Workout in chapter 2). It may help you in your intercession to stand, walk about, lie prostrate, kneel, etc.

5 mins   Praise God at the end for all that has been accomplished through your prayers even though you cannot see them apart from in the 'spirit realm'.

DAY 5

BIBLE STUDY

25 mins   Read Daniel 9.

1 What was the situation at this time in the nation of Israel?
2 Where in the book of Jeremiah does he prophesy that Israel will be seventy years in captivity?
3 Daniel saw that the end of these seventy years was fast approaching — what did he do? Did he sit back and wait to see if God would do it or did he become part of the answer himself? What can we learn from this?

160

4   Although Daniel was a righteous man, he identified in prayer with the sins of his nation. What can we learn from this in our own times of prayer for our nations?

5   Read verse 18. Ask God to speak to you through this verse. Write down what you receive.

6   Read verses 20–2. God breaks in supernaturally during his prayer time. He gives him 'insight and understanding'. Ask God to give you 'insight and understanding' for the situation for which you are praying and interceding.

5 mins   Go for a short walk with God. Revise your memory verses as you walk (Luke 11:9–10).

DAY 6

10 mins   Read Acts 1:8 and Mark 16:15. You may not physically be able to go into different parts of the world to preach the gospel – but you can be a part of reaching other nations through your prayers. Spend a few minutes in prayer asking God to lay one or more nations on your heart. Write down the nations for which you'd like to pray. Write down (or make a note to find out) any information you have on the spiritual state of these nations.

15 mins   Lay each one before the Lord and intercede for them. Pray for the following in each nation:

1   The ruling authorities
2   The Church
3   Missionaries or Christian organisations
4   The poor and needy

Pray in English and/or pray in tongues. Again, ask the Holy Spirit, who knows all things, to intercede through you. Don't be surprised if you weep, feel pain or groan before God. When you finish, write down anything you saw or felt as you prayed.

5 mins   Read Luke 10:2. Ask God to send more workers into His harvest field.

161

DAY 7

5 mins   Meditate on Matthew 6:20. Write down what you receive through this scripture.

10 mins   Read Ezekiel 22:30. This passage explains that God is constantly looking for people to intercede and stand in the gap before Him. Read and pray the words of the following song to God and spend time interceding on behalf of your nation.

HEAL OUR NATION

Lord we long for you to move in power,
There's a hunger deep within our hearts,
To see healing in our nation,
Send your Spirit to revive us.

Heal our nation,
Heal our nation,
Heal our nation,
Pour out your Spirit on this land.

Lord we hear your Spirit coming closer,
A mighty wave to break upon our land,
Bringing justice and forgiveness,
God we cry to you, 'Revive us.'

Ray Goudie, Dave Morgan, Townend, Steve Bankhead.
Copyright 1986. Thank you Music

10 mins   Go out for a walk with God. Ask Him how He feels about your nation and the world around you. Write down what He says and ask God to help you feel what He's feeling.

5 mins   Thank the Lord for the privilege of being able to work with Him in the area of prayer. Thank Him for all you have learned this week and ask Him to take you into deeper realms of prayer and intercession. Thank Him that He can use your prayers — no matter how simple they are. Ask His forgiveness for your lack of prayer in the past and commit yourself to going deeper with God in prayer in the future.

New Generation Ministries

New Generation Ministries is led by Ray and Nancy Goudie. In 1980 they were the leaders of the music ministry team of British Youth for Christ. During this time, Ray and Nancy formed the band Heartbeat and left the salaried staff of BYFC to establish a 'faith-based' ministry involved in evangelism, training, worship, media, mission and church planting.

In 1985, God gave them a deep desire in their hearts for revival and a strong conviction that a new outpouring of His Spirit was going to take place in the nations of the world. During this time they also brought this prophetic message to millions of people as they released singles that broke into the secular charts. They appeared on many radio and television shows including the BBC's chart programme *Top of the Pops*. As their ministry continued to develop and in line with their growing vision to see a new generation reached for God, they changed their name in 1989 to New Generation Ministries. With Heartbeat finishing in 1991 a new chapter had begun, with God promising even greater blessing as they continued to bring the good news to this needy and hurting generation.

Part of their ministry is the recruiting, training and placing of young bands/teams to work alongside churches in evangelism, discipleship and church planting. NGM's production company, Ultra Music, is currently working in their twenty-four-track studio to produce songs that will again be released in the secular market. The NGM bands, 65dBA, Jimmy Ragstaff, re:fresh and Rhythmworks, are already making a great impact throughout

Europe and the USA. Albums of the bands are available from NGM.

If you want to join our mailing list or receive more information on NGM, please write to:

NGM, Severn Ridge, 29 Gloucester Road, Almondsbury, Bristol BS12 4HH.